# EL SALVADOR

## DANCE OF THE DEATH SQUADS, 1980–1992

AL J. VENTER

Pen & Sword
MILITARY

First published in Great Britain in 2017 by
PEN AND SWORD MILITARY
*an imprint of*
Pen and Sword Books Ltd
47 Church Street
Barnsley
South Yorkshire S70 2AS

Copyright © Al J. Venter, 2017

ISBN 978 1 52670 814 4

The right of Al J. Venter to be identified as the author of this work
has been asserted in accordance with the Copyright, Designs and Patents Act 1988.

A CIP record for this book is available from the British Library All rights reserved.
No part of this book may be reproduced or transmitted in any form or by any means, electronic or
mechanical including photocopying, recording or by any information storage and retrieval system,
without permission from the Publisher in writing.

Every reasonable effort has been made to trace copyright holders of material reproduced in this book,
but if any have been inadvertently overlooked the publishers will be pleased to hear from them.

Typeset by Aura Technology and Software Services, India
Printed and bound by CPI Group (UK) Ltd, Croydon, CR0 4YY

Pen & Sword Books Ltd incorporates the imprints of Pen & Sword
Archaeology, Atlas, Aviation, Battleground, Discovery, Family History, History, Maritime, Military,
Naval, Politics, Railways, Select, Social History, Transport, True Crime, Claymore Press, Frontline Books,
Leo Cooper, Praetorian Press, Remember When, Seaforth Publishing and Wharncliffe.

*For a complete list of Pen and Sword titles please contact*
Pen and Sword Books Limited
47 Church Street, Barnsley, South Yorkshire, S70 2AS, England
email: enquiries@pen-and-sword.co.uk
website: www.pen-and-sword.co.uk

# CONTENTS

|     |     |
| --- | --- |
| Timeline | 5 |
| Introduction | 11 |
| Prologue | 15 |
| 1. Background | 31 |
| 2. A Dirty, Distant War | 36 |
| 3. First Impressions | 41 |
| 4. Covering the War | 52 |
| 5. More American Involvement | 57 |
| 6. The Legend of the Bearded One | 66 |
| 7. Military Advisory Group | 75 |
| 8. Central American Crisis | 85 |
| 9. No Man's Land | 96 |
| 10. US Military Assistance Command | 112 |
| Notes | 122 |
| Bibliography | 123 |
| Acknowledgements | 125 |
| About the Author | 127 |

FMLN combatant, Museum of the Revolution, Perquín, El Salvador. (Photo Linda Hess Miller)

# TIMELINE

**1524**

Spanish adventurer Pedro de Alvarado conquers El Salvador.

**1540**

Indigenous resistance finally crushed and El Salvador becomes a Spanish colony.

**1821**

El Salvador gains independence from Spain. Conflict ensues over territory's incorporation into Mexican empire under Creole general Agustin de Iturbide.

**1823**

El Salvador becomes part of the United Provinces of Central America, which also includes Costa Rica, Guatemala, Honduras and Nicaragua.

**1840**

El Salvador becomes fully independent, following the dissolution of the United Provinces of Central America.

**1859–63**

President Gerardo Barrios introduces coffee growing.

**1932**

Some 30,000 people are killed during the suppression of a peasant uprising led by Agustín Farabundo Martí Rodriguez.

Right-wing National Conciliation Party (PCN) comes to power after a military coup.

**1969**

El Salvador attacks and fights a brief war with Honduras following the eviction of thousands of illegal Salvadoran immigrants from Honduras.

Statue to national hero Gerardo Barrios, president of El Salvador, 1859–63. (Photo Brigadier044)

## 1970

The leftist Farabundo Martí Liberation People's Forces (Fuerzas Populares de Liberación Farabundo Martí, or FPL) is formed on 1 April to take up arms against the El Salvador regime. Also formed this year is the People's Revolutionary Army (Ejército Revolucionario del Pueblo, or ERP), another militant leftist organization.

## 1977

Guerrilla activities by FPL and ERP intensify amid reports of increased human-rights violations by government troops and death squads. General Carlos Humberto Romero is elected president.

## 1979–81

Around 30,000 people are killed by army-backed, right-wing death squads.

## 1979

General Romero is ousted in a coup by reformist officers, who install a military–civilian junta, but this fails to curb army-backed political violence.

## 1980

March – Archbishop of San Salvador and human rights campaigner Óscar Romero is assassinated. José Napoleón Duarte becomes the first civilian president since 1931.

October – The left-wing Farabundo Martí National Liberation Front (Frente Farabundo Martí para la Liberación Nacional, or FMLN), an umbrella group for five leftist guerrilla organizations, including ERP and FPL, is officially formed on the 10th of the month.

## 1981
France and Mexico recognize the FMLN as a legitimate political entity. The US continues to assist the El Salvadoran government, whose army continues to back right-wing death squads.

## 1982
The extreme right-wing National Republican Alliance, ARENA (Alianza Republicana Nacionalista) wins parliamentary elections that are marred by violence.

## 1984
Duarte wins the presidential election.

## 1986
Duarte begins his quest for a negotiated settlement with the FMLN.

## 1989
FMLN attacks intensify. Another ARENA candidate, Alfredo Cristiani, is voted president in elections, which are widely believed to have been rigged. A time of peace and natural disasters.

## 1991
The FMLN is recognized as a political party. The government and the FMLN sign a UN-sponsored peace accord.

## 1993
The government declares an amnesty for those implicated by a UN-sponsored commission into human rights atrocities.

## 1994
ARENA candidate Armando Calderón Sol is elected president.

## 1997

The FMLN makes progress in parliamentary elections. Leftist Hector Silva is elected mayor of San Salvador.

## 1999

ARENA candidate Francisco Flores beats former guerrilla Facundo Guardado in presidential elections.

## 2001

January–February – Massive earthquakes kill 1,200 people and render another million homeless.

## 2002

July – A US court holds two retired, US-based Salvadoran army generals responsible for civil war atrocities, ordering them to compensate the victims who had lodged the case.

## 2003

August – 360 Salvadoran troops are despatched to Iraq.

December – El Salvador, along with Honduras, Nicaragua, Guatemala, agrees on a free-trade agreement with the US. The government ratifies the pact in December 2004.

## 2004

March – ARENA candidate Elías Antonio 'Tony' Saca wins the presidential elections.

## 2005

March – An Organization of American States (OAS) human rights court votes to re-open an investigation into the 1981 massacre of hundreds of peasant farmers in the village of El Mozote, regarded as one of the worst atrocities of the civil war.

October – Thousands flee as the Santa Ana, or Ilamatepec, volcano, erupts. Days later scores of people are killed as tropical storm *Stan* makes landfall.

*Timeline*

US Secretary of Defense Donald Rumsfeld thanking Salvadoran military leaders for their steadfastness in Iraq as a coalition partner. (Photo James M. Bowman)

## 2006

March – El Salvador is the first Central American country to implement a regional free trade agreement with the US.

April – El Salvador and neighbouring Honduras inaugurate their newly defined border. The countries fought over the disputed frontier in 1969.

## 2007

January – Twenty-one inmates are killed in a riot at a maximum-security prison west of the capital.

February – Three members of the governing ARENA party are murdered in Guatemala. There are suspicions that an organized crime syndicate is behind the killings.

## 2008

January – More than 400 judges hold a street protest over corruption allegations made against four of their colleagues.

## 2009
January – The former FMLN rebel movement emerges as the largest party in parliamentary elections, although short of a majority. This is seen as a preparation for presidential elections. in March.

February – The ruling party ARENA wins the largest number of seats in local elections, despite the polls favouring the opposition FMLN.

March – Former Marxist rebel Mauricio Funes of the FMLN party wins the presidential elections, marking the first time in two decades that a leftist president has been elected.

June – Mauricio Funes is sworn in as president. He restores diplomatic relations with Cuba.

November – More than 140 people are killed and thousands left homeless in mudslides and floods.

## 2010
June – Fourteen people are killed in two attacks by suspected gang members on public buses in the capital, San Salvador.

## 2011
September – The US adds El Salvador and Belize to its list of countries considered to be major producers or transit routes of illegal drugs.

October – Torrential rains cause flooding across Central America, killing several people in El Salvador.

December – The government apologizes for the civil war massacre of more than 1,000 people in the town of El Mozote.

## 2012
March – Funes's government suffers a setback in parliamentary polls, which give the right wing a narrow victory.

# INTRODUCTION

Every book deserves what the scribbling community likes to refer to as a 'peg on which to hang your story', as does this one. I can think of no better way of placing before you a few comments about a book written some years about the war in El Salvador by someone who was very much involved, not as a combatant, but rather, as an observer. His name is Joseph Frazier, author of *El Salvador Could Be Like That*, a memoir of war and journalism based on reporting in that country between 1979 and 1986 when hostilities were at their mind-bendingly worst.[1]

Raised in Eugene, Oregon, Joe Frazier was well qualified to judge what was going on. As a United States Marine, he had already spent thirteen months in another war on the far side of the globe: Vietnam. There were obviously parallels. Thereafter, he resumed his studies in journalism, history and languages at the University of Oregon.

As he says in his own introduction to the book:

> I covered El Salvador from 1979–1986 – the worst of the war years – for the Associated Press. In addition to wartime coverage, I visited several times later for the AP, and after retirement took solo road trips down from Oregon in 2009 and 2011.
>
> My memoir is a ground's-eye view of the El Salvador war and of what it did to the peasants, the soldiers, the school kids, the union leaders, the shopkeepers, the fishermen and artisans, the parish priests – the everyday, unremarkable people who often wound up in unmarked graves and on the edit-room floor. It is also a look at the politics and economics and social history that underpinned the conflict.
>
> I believe the journalists I worked with there in those years were among the finest anywhere. Too many of them died trying to get the story out. Many of the living will stroke a greying whisker or two and say, 'No, it wasn't that way at all, it was this way, or this.' But these are my recollections.

Scott Wallace, author of *The Unconquered: In Search of the Amazon's Last Uncontacted Tribes* takes up the cudgels. I quote directly from comments he made in an amazon.com review of the book, for which he gave five stars. A former foreign correspondent based in El Salvador and Nicaragua, Wallace, like Frazier, covered Central America and the Caribbean during the tumultuous 1980s for *Newsweek*, CBS News and others.

As he says, precious few books and memoirs have been written about the events that unfolded in Central America in the 1980s. A full-blown civil war was underway in El Salvador and, just across the Gulf of Fonseca in neighbouring Nicaragua, the United States was supporting a proxy uprising against the leftist Sandinista government:

> For an entire generation of journalists who had grown up watching images of the Vietnam War on the nightly news, Central America seemed to offer a similar promise of the Big Story – the twisted imperatives of empire trumping concerns for human rights amid the clatter of helicopters and the snap of bullets on a jungle landscape.
>
> It seemed to many that El Salvador would go the way of Vietnam, with US involvement escalating from initial training by mobile Special Forces teams to an eventual direct intervention to prop up a corrupt, brutal

Arrest of a mechanic for not carrying an ID card. (Photo John Hoagland)

and seemingly intransigent regime incapable of reform. But the reforms did come, albeit slowly and not always prettily, alongside a sophisticated post-Vietnam counterinsurgency campaign. The US never did intervene directly and El Salvador eventually slid out of the headlines as the war neared its end in the early 1990s.

Few people born after the mid-1980s even know that [Washington] was in the 1980s heavily invested in two proxy wars – in El Salvador and Nicaragua – conflicts that ultimately left tens of thousands of dead and produced hundreds of thousands of refugees, many of whom ended up in the United States.

As he indicates, Joe Frazier seeks to rectify this collective amnesia with his book, *El Salvador Could Be Like That*. Wallace adds:

It is a welcome effort and a welcome addition to the literature of war reportage. El Salvador was the cauldron where the careers of many reporters were forged. Unlike Nicaragua, where the Contra rebels failed to penetrate the urban population centres and where correspondents had to make a concerted effort to find the war in the deep countryside, El Salvador offered a gritty and grim tableau of violence at every turn. Bodies turned up everywhere and anywhere.

As Frazier states, 'the war was everywhere and nowhere.' The result could be at moments terrifying, exhilarating, and tedious for young reporters seeking to find their way in a morass of ever-shifting shadows. At the very least, there was always a certain, subliminal fear lurking just over one's shoulder. Many fine journalists died while bearing witness to the events in El Salvador and Central America, including Frazier's own wife, Linda, who fell victim to a bomb planted by Sandinista state security at a rebel news conference on the Nicaragua–Costa Rica border.

Douglas Grant Mine, another amazon.com reader, made the comment about the work that

the main reason this is such a good and illuminating read about 'the Tom Thumb of the Americas' during its horrible and heroic revolutionary era is because Frazier really cared.

Not about which camp was going to come away with the geopolitical prize, but about the country folk and city folk, the shopkeepers and dirt farmers and bus drivers and coffee pickers and shine boys and *pupusa* [tortilla] flippers whose sons and brothers (sisters, too, in the case of the rebel army) were killing and getting killed along the road leading from a quasi-feudal repressive system of economy and politics to an approximation of democratic modernity.

It's a great story, one that's founded on the idiosyncratic verve and vitality of Salvadorans themselves. There's abundant discussion as to why *los Guanacos* [moniker derived from the name of a species of camelid] are so inimitably like they are. Maybe their industriousness and stoicism and good humour and resilience derive from being jammed into the smallest nation of the continental Americas, the overcrowded condition giving rise to a cogent mix of competition and cooperation.

Whatever the reason, even though politicos and pawn-movers and pundits far-off were speculating, while *el Pulgarcito* [Tom Thumb] bled, as to what El Salvador 'could be like,' the truth was that this diminutive larger-than-life land of commonplace marvels was, and is, one of a kind.

Salvadoran troops of the special reaction forces (Fuerzas Especailizadas de Reacción).
(Photo President's Office, El Salvador)

# PROLOGUE

Dana Drenkowski flew more than 200 combat missions in B-52 bombers and Phantom F4s for the United States Air Force in Vietnam. Years later, after a spell as a mercenary in Rhodesia's guerrilla war of the 1970s, he found himself in El Salvador's war – two tours of duty flying combat in the Cessna A-37 Dragonfly, Douglas C-47 Skytrain, Bell UH-1 Iroquois 'Huey' helicopter, and the Cessna O-2 Skymaster against the rebel Faribundo Martí National Liberation Front, the FMLN. His career throughout, as one of his protagonists appropriately described it, was 'chequered', ending as it did as a DA in Stockton California, before retiring in 2016. One of his pals with whom he had seen a bit of action described Drenkowski as 'a modest man, dark-haired and strung tight'.

Drenkowski is not sure of the exact date that he first arrived in San Salvador, but it was in the early 1980s. As he recalls, he was met by a friend who gave him some good advice about life in that wartime capital. The first subject touched on concerned roadblocks, between the country's only international airport and the Sheraton Hotel in San Salvador.

'First Dana,' our pal told him, 'there are four different agencies you need to know about. The national police, who work as a paramilitary force and from which organization comes forth most of the allegations of human rights violations. They are of course, uniformed and not military, so you will recognize them easily.

'Next is the Salvo military, who wear camouflage uniforms with military ranks, unit patches, and web gear. Again, no problem to recognize and no real threat to you as an American, particularly if you are wearing some kind of military gear yourself.'

To which Drenkowski retorted, 'I understand the military and police, old pal, but why the emphasis on recognizing them and the uniforms?'

'Because you may get stopped at roadblocks and then you have to be ready to respond with one of two actions when you recognize who the blockers are.' The friend explained that the requisite responses were to present ID cards or present guns with which to fight. 'With the military and police, ID cards or passports will get you through the roadblock,' the friend added.

*El Salvador*

Dana Drenkowski at Reese Air Force Base, Lubbock, Texas, 1969. (Al J. Venter collection)

'So what are the other two groups and how do I recognize them?' Drenkowski queried, somewhat confused.

'The guerrillas, amigo – the FMLN! They are all in civilian clothes, such as jeans and T-shirts.' He added, however, that it was usually quite easy to tell who they were by the military web gear they always wore.

'That is their identification to themselves and to the rest of El Salvador that they are members of a fighting unit and that is important. If you have to fight, expect that they know how to use their weapons and how to manoeuvre. You understand what I am talking about, Dana?'

The American nodded before his friend went on.

'So, *tu entiendes* [you understand], the rest are bandits – dressed the same as the Gs [as locals referred to the guerrillas] but without the web gear. And if it comes to the point where you have to fight them, they are generally easy to take out if you are a trained military man.'

'So, what this means to me is that every roadblock manned by people in civilian clothes, I might have to fight, no matter what the odds – nothing much to think about then?' Drenkowski concluded.

'Well,' our buddy responded, 'you might have somewhat of a chance of being taken alive by the FMLN Gs as opposed to the bandits. They could regard you as good trading material; but you'd have to expect torture and perhaps execution anyway.'

The next item on our friend's agenda was self-protection.

'Dana, we do go out on the town to restaurants, movies, tourist sites, and whorehouses. You'll always be spotted as a *Norte Americano* wherever you go, so you'll be targeted by the Gs working undercover or the bandits who are just about everywhere. That means you carry your gun whenever you go anywhere! Some of us – and those honchos of course –- have their guns in belt holsters under a loose shirt that is pretty common to these tropics.'

He went on to explain that most of those who might be needing what he referred to as 'protection' liked to carry their weapons in specially designed carry-bags, called 'fag bags' by one and all.

'They are preferable because you can take along a large gun like a Colt .45 auto rather than a smaller hide-out .38 revolver or a 9mm handgun.'

As a result, one of the first things Drenkowski did when he arrived in the country was to go out and buy a Walther .380 PPK and a 9mm Smith & Wesson compact pistol. These were in addition to the two .45 ACPs (automatic Colt pistol),

Drenkowski preparing for A-37 operations, Ilopango. (Al J. Venter collection)

one full-size, the other in the standard short-barrelled version that he brought with him from the States.

Drenkowski gives an insight into his El Salvador experience:

> I sometimes carried the 9mm or the .380, but I usually brought the .45 Colt along in one of the little carry bags I acquired in a stall off San Salvador's main drag. I felt that it would be more decisive in a gun fight.
>
> My contact at the United States embassy in San Salvador told me that he and the American military advisors found their jobs almost impossible due to Congressional limitations about being on combat ops with the El Salvador military. They had no idea what was really working or not working in combat, whether the El Salvador military leaders were following the laws of warfare and if millions of dollars in American aid was actually making it to the fight instead of lining someone's pockets somewhere else. Or, something that bothered a lot of people, possibly ending up in a Swiss bank account.
>
> In part, I was looked upon as a solution to that problem. With no official US contacts, I was merely a civilian 'mercenary' who could go anywhere and do just about anything without violating US legal restrictions.

*Prologue*

Included among my first obligations was a series of introductions to various senior officers of the El Salvador air force, the Fuerza Aerea El Salvador (FAS), with whom I'd be flying and working while there. I don't recall anyone prominent except the irascible Colonel Bustillo, a larger than life character who ran the air force with an iron fist. Difficult to please, he was well liked and respected by the rest of the FAS. My ticket into his office came from my embassy contact – the one who had asked me to head south to this Caribbean nation some weeks before. That, of course, kind of fingered me. My friend was widely known in El Salvador to be linked to American intelligence and, naturally, that meant to the FAS that I was 'Intel' as well. They weren't all that far off either. As mentioned earlier, I was sent to El Salvador to observe, train and report back to United States intelligence services and to Congress, effectively a sounding board for the folks back home to tell them exactly what was going on in that dirty, distant war.

For all that, I was never a true-to-life, card-carrying member of any of Washington's three-letter agencies, as some of those with whom I came into contact believed I was.

'Feel free to fly anything we have and participate in any combat operations you choose to,' were the final words addressed to me by Colonel Bustillo as his aide took me out to meet the people who mattered at the country's main air force base at Ilopango.

It didn't take long. The entire FAS had the equivalent of one or two US Air Force squadrons and about seventy pilots in all. They welcomed me, but over the next few days while there, kind of feeling my way and not achieving much because of language problems, I could tell they were, if not stand-offish, then certainly wary of my presence. In their minds, there was probably good reason: the 'higher-ups' recognized me as some kind of intelligence agent and, I suppose, they didn't really trust me. The word must surely have filtered down the ranks.

As expected, I was issued with a military ID card, which plainly identified me as a US embassy asset – a certain death warrant if I was ever captured, because the only American embassy person who might be out on combat operations would have to be a military advisor or a CIA agent. In the minds of most of the locals with whom I associated, just about everything to do with American intelligence had to be CIA, though many American security types actually worked for the Defence Intelligence Agency, or DIA, the National

On landing back at Ilopango, and taxiing in to the chocks, I found the commander of the squadron waiting for me. He was quite excited when he came up to me after I'd clambered down from the cockpit.

'Are you a member of the famous Air Force Thunderbirds?' he asked, his voice an octave or two higher than usual.

'Why no,' I answered, more than a little surprised. 'What makes you think so?'

'The flight leader called me,' he answered cagily. 'He told me about the amazing stunt flying you were doing in that A-37! You must be one of America's best pilots sent here to help us out.'

I should have been flattered, but in truth I wasn't. I had to explain to him that I wasn't a Thunderbird, nor had I ever served in that remarkable squadron.

'I'm just an average pilot, I said. What I did with those barrel rolls was what any US Air Force fighter pilot can do – it's quite normal in our air force.'

I'm still not sure if he believed me, but my reputation in the FAS was securely established from then on in by a few moments of boredom en route to the target. And curiously, my other, more sinister reputation was also enhanced, that I was some kind of secret agent sent to spy on them. Only someone so well trained as a fighter pilot could have managed what only James Bond might have been able to do. Or so they believed, and I wasn't going to argue.

I was immediately offered any of the French-built Dassault Ouragan fighter aircraft to fly whenever I wanted. But they were single-seaters, and since my Spanish language skills were abysmal – I'd have to talk to controllers and forward air controllers in that language – I did not feel comfortable about jumping into that plane's cockpit on my own. In any event, it was early days, and I needed somebody who was bilingual to tell me where the new 'unbriefed' target would be or what to communicate with the tower on our way home when it came to landing instructions.

Not long afterwards, my embassy friend advised me that American reconnaissance missions were being routinely flown over El Salvador, photographing every single yard of that country. There wasn't a house, shed, building, barn or lean-to that didn't end up on our files. Everything was recorded and, where possible, government and local records were searched to establish exactly who lived in every one of them.

Disused El Salvador air force (FAS) Dassault Ouragan, Ilopango. (Photo aeroprints.com)

As the guerrillas took over an area, they would drive out some inhabitants so that they could move into their houses or buildings for shelter. Reconnaissance flights included infra-red cameras, so it was easy to see when someone moved into an otherwise 'abandoned' structure.

In turn, that led to further investigation of that building, or sets of buildings, and it made it easy to find the Gs whenever they moved into a specific neighbourhood. Air strikes would soon follow, sometimes within twenty-four hours of the Gs moving in. Clearly, the ability to mobilize those resources had a marked effect on guerrilla ability to fight effectively. On top of which, the Gs had absolutely no idea how we had established where they were.

There was an additional benefit. It did not take long for the guerrillas to become totally paranoid. Always eager to terrorize the locals, they now believed some of the locals were informing on them, or that their own ranks had been infiltrated by our agents. In fact, our systematic methods had no need to rely on informants to achieve results.

Therefore, it wasn't long before the FMLN began hunting down 'suspects'. This in turn poisoned the relationships between the G 'fish' and the peasant 'sea' that Mao Zedong said the insurgents need to cultivate to succeed in any insurgency struggle.

I began flying everything the El Salvador air force had, as long as it had an extra seat for the more fluent Spanish–English speaker.

Days consisted of going to briefings, flying and debriefing, then heading back 'home' to the Sheraton Hotel. I actually felt safer during the day while working at Ilopango air base, surrounded by hundreds of heavily armed military personnel, coupled with strong defences around the base. Back at the hotel, there was always the possibility of a rocket-propelled grenade, such as an RPG-7, being fired into the rooms occupied by my fellow 'mercenaries'.

Flying combat in Salvador was one of the easier aerial-combat situations I'd found myself in. Unlike other places, El Salvador was simple to navigate, mainly because there are five large volcanoes scattered about this Massachusetts-sized country. All of them were more or less active, some emitting sulphur gases, others more quiescent, depending on the month or year. One would move from volcano to volcano, or offset to one side or another. Instead of triangulation, there were always five peaks sticking up, even on cloudy days, and if the clouds reached high enough to cover the volcano tops, there was always a smoke trail rising above the cloud bank to show where the active ones were.

And at night, there was the smoke, not really noticeable until you were just about on top of it and a sudden, pungent, sulphurous odour told you were directly over a volcano, if you knew which ones were smoking, you knew where you were, even without any direct vision.

Suspicions about my active role persisted, and I found myself sometimes excluded from certain briefings or discussions. It was polite, but obvious that there were things going on that they did not want outsiders to know about. And I was that outsider.

Until one notable day. Shortly after arriving for a mission at Ilopango, the base exploded in a frenzy of excitement, more so than I'd seen for any other mission during my recent work at the base.

'What is going on,' I asked one of the passing pilots, who was practically running to an intelligence briefing, one of those from which I was excluded.

'SAM-7s!' he exclaimed, referring to man-portable air defence systems, or MANPADS. It was obvious the man was worried. So, it seemed, was virtually every other pilot or aircrew member on the base.

*Prologue*

'We just received intelligence that the Sandinistas are smuggling Soviet ground-to-air missiles into El Salvador! The FAS is grounded until further notice!'

Unquestionably, MANPADS are a game-changer in any guerrilla conflict. Aircraft most capable of combating an insurgency are customarily slower and fly lower than the types of aircraft found in most other conventional air force inventories.

The SAM-7, taken into El Salvador by FMLN cadres, we soon discovered was the latest generation anti-aircraft missile available in the Third World. It was like the American AIM-9 Sidewinder, with its shoulder-fired version

SA-7 man-portable air-defence systems (MANPADS) training in the US. (Photo DVIDSHUB)

known as the Redeye. I had first encountered SAM-7s in Vietnam. When these missiles were first introduced against a US Air Force that wasn't prepared for them, they shot down several helicopters and even AC-130 gunships, probably the most expensive high-tech weapons being flown over the Ho Chi Minh Trail at the time.

It took several months for both tactics and technology to reduce the MANPADs to just another threat, little different from other weapons such as radar-guided, computer-controlled, fully automatic, anti-aircraft cannons we had been encountering for years.

When the FAS personnel emerged from their Intel briefing, all looked, if not frightened, then extremely concerned. I finally took a squadron commander aside and told him I had been flying against these missiles during all my F-4 missions in Southeast Asia, all 165 of them, with no problems. I knew exactly how to manoeuvre to counter their threat, I told him. Also, how to avoid them, and what to do when fired upon.

Within minutes, I was hauled before Colonel Bustillo, who wanted confirmation from me that I knew all about these missiles. I declared confidently that in the US Air Force and Navy aviation we flew against them all the time, going back to when I was on my second tour in 1972–73.

When asked, I told him that not only would I be prepared to teach his pilots, but I would also show his guys how to out-manoeuvre them when fired upon, and how to keep away from them before being fired upon.

I had never seen an entire air force staff assembled quite so quickly. Within fifteen minutes, I was led onto a stage in front of the entire FAS flying establishment of all seventy pilots and additional aircrew, including door gunners. I barely had time to prepare what I was going to tell them, except that I had to give them the full nine yards and hoped I wasn't going to forget and leave out anything significant.

Within a couple of hours, I'd given everybody the full lowdown on Soviet SAMs, and more importantly, at what altitudes they should fly, how to manoeuvre once a missile was spotted coming in, what speeds to maintain, and so on. Slow movers like the C-47s were toast if they were low enough and the enemy got a good bead on them, but that was only part of it.

Among other important background detail was the fact that Soviet batteries were exclusive to the missiles. Moreover, they were delicate, vulnerable to jarring and erratic under tropical conditions. Once the missile had been switched on, the operator had only a few minutes' usable time to do the necessary. If not fired, the battery and the entire missile system became inoperative. In true Soviet fashion, spare batteries very rarely came with the missiles.

Also, being heat-seekers – like our own Sidewinders – their tracker systems were designed to lock onto heat sources, the exhausts of piston and jet engines. Simple deflectors, affixed to exhausts that forced hot air upward and into the downwash of helicopter engines, for instance, would dissipate such heat sources, enough, at least, to dislocate a missile's seeker system.

The FAS went from a shutdown mode back to full operations within a day. Also, the confidence of the pilots was given a welcome boost. And so, by explaining to those pilots how easy it was to fly with the threat of SAM-7s in their areas of operations, I suddenly was no longer that dreaded 'spy' in their midst, but one of them. Nor was I ever again excluded from briefings.

With my new-found respect, both from flying skills as well as my apparent self-promoted 'heroism' of having seen and out-manoeuvred several supersonic anti-aircraft missiles in my career, I felt I could begin teaching human rights and the laws of land warfare to my fellow FAS aviators.

We had a few more 'all-FAS' training sessions scheduled, and this time I gave more prepared briefings about the subject: the Geneva Convention, The Hague Protocols, and the Geneva Protocols. I reminded the pilots, many of whom had received training from the Argentine and Chilean air forces, that some members of those armed services were now concerned about being prosecuted for violations committed during the 'dirty wars' against their own insurgencies.

At the same time, I made the pilots consider their families, and how it might feel if they had to worry about being arrested by a follow-on government, or by international human rights enforcers, even twenty or thirty years in the future, should they have committed any violations. Telling them what it was like for their friends in those other forces to worry about that 'knock on the door', and how former Nazis even thirty-five years later were still being hunted, made an impact. I ignored the uncomfortable fact that most Communist war criminals and human rights violators were unaffected – and are still unaffected to this day.

Disused FAS Fouga CM-170R Magister, Ilopango. (Photo aeroprints.com)

As a lawyer, I could tell them about the law. As a combat fighter pilot, I could tell them how they could still do their jobs effectively enough to win the war, yet stay within those legal guidelines. I gave them examples of how I did it, as well as hypotheticals, taking questions at all points. And I taught them that they would have to be brave enough to say 'No' to some requests or orders from the ground soldiers who might ask them to hit questionable targets.

I was now a part of the FAS and felt accepted, so I could speak my mind. It was accepted by all.

Curiously, those same Soviet ground-to-air missiles didn't turn out to be such a threat during the months I worked with FAS. Either the Intel was wrong, or the battery and tropical-vulnerability issues conspired to keep the SAM-7s non-operational for quite a while.

On the air base, things constantly changed. When we had increased tempo operations, I didn't go back to the Sheraton after hours. Instead, I slept on the bare army cots or floors with the rest of the pilots on standby, waiting for missions, and eating with them nothing but beans and rice.

On one of those times, the FMLN 'probed' the base with a small ground attack. Our .50-calibre machine guns and the aggressive shooting from combat units chased them off before we could get aerial assets out to fix and destroy them.

That night, on short notice, I found myself flying with nothing but two door gunners in one of their gunships, a UH-1 Huey gunship with wide-mounted guns alongside the doors of the chopper. The usual 'guy in the other seat', who spoke fluent Spanish and English, was not required, as I didn't need to worry about landing instructions or combat issues while handling on my own whatever came up locally.

It was surreal. A very clear night, with a two-thirds moon, no mist, and not much volcanic activity to mess up the view. The gunners tuned our radios to a Miami Cuban radio station playing popular music, both Cuban and American. There we were, circling Ilopango, some miles out, with infra-red scopes looking for insurgents, finally zeroing in on a hot-spot in the 'boonies' [short for boondock, a corruption of a Philippine word *bundok*, used by Americans to mean a remote or out-of-the-way place] only to find that we had exposed a secret Salvadoran military patrol in its ambush site trying to catch the guerrilla enemy infiltrating on another probe.

They waved in the dark. There was enough light to identify them, so we moved on, hoping the FMLN hadn't noticed our sudden swooping in on a 'gun run' that went dry at the last second.

I was advised some years later that after my legal briefings, the FAS was never successfully challenged or accused by international observers of any real violations of human rights, contrary to some issues prior. It became one of my prouder 'merc' [mercenary] moments in life.

And yet they were still able to make a major difference in the war. Big jet-fighter planes, until the later development of high-precision weaponry, were often counter-productive in insurgency warfare, where low, slow, and extremely accurate weapons were needed to do the job. People with the American military, however, helped the El Salvador air force get it right, with the delivery of C-47 and helicopter gunships, slower jets like the A-37s, and many other recon platforms.

What was significant about the war in El Salvador, throughout the years that it lasted, was that the media and numerous American and European politicians

FAS Bell UH-1 Iroquois 'Huey' gunship. (Photo El Salvador army)

castigated the San Salvador government for human rights abuses. In other words, in its most simplistic form, the 'Right' was evil, while rebel forces on the 'Left' could do nothing wrong.

The 'Right' may have been brutal in its fighting, but the Leftist-Marxists were equally brutal in their approach. For example, one constantly hears about rightist 'death squads', yet the Marxist groups always had their own death squads running full steam as well.

The difference was primarily in what happened later. After fighting for control, the Right eased up and had no agenda to fundamentally change human nature, unlike the Left, who, once the war was over, resorted to the continuous murder of those people who would not, could not, or were perceived as being unable to fundamentally change their nature.

# 1. BACKGROUND

At the strategic level, the insurgency in El Salvador began in the early 1970s, a time of great dissent within many countries in Central and South America. It was also a time when Cuba was pushing hard for various radical political movements to strike out, in bids to create a vast socialist region within and adjacent to the Caribbean belt.

In El Salvador's case, according to a thesis written by United States Army Major Paul P. Cale, and quoted in its entirety by *Small Wars Journal*,[1] since the beginning of what was to become a full-on civil war, the opposition's strategy of accomplishing their objective of restructuring the government was altered from time to time in recognition of changing political-military conditions.

An historic photo of early Central American dissidents who gave their names to the revolutions that followed. Augusto Sandino of Nicaragua is standing with crossed legs and a cigar, while El Salvador's Agustín Farabundo Martí Rodriguez is seated right.

In 1979, General Carlos Humberto Romero was brought to power by the military because they thought he could maintain the status quo in El Salvador. There was growing unrest in the country, both by landless *campesinos* (peasant farmers) and a new breed of young military officers, who were genuinely concerned with what they perceived was the old style of government led by senior military officers.

Opposition to military governments during the 1970s was unrelenting, causing widespread civil unrest that was continually answered with brutal repression by the government. Dissatisfaction continued to build during this period. At the same time, the opposition gained strength by observing events in neighbouring Nicaragua.

After 1977, opposition parties within El Salvador abandoned their reliance on elections. Concurrently, the Salvadoran government became more savage in its repression of the opposition in an attempt to stop the growing number of demonstrations, strikes and protests.

Victory of the Sandinistas over the Somoza regime in Nicaragua helped spread the opposition's message that the time was right to topple the military regime in El Salvador. The evolving situation in El Salvador at the end of the decade provided another opportunity for the expansion of communism into Central America.

The Soviet Union with it loyal revolutionary comrades in Cuba, and thereafter in Nicaragua, decided to accept the challenge and back the growing insurgent movement. Meanwhile, political leaders in the United States understood that if the Salvadoran government did not reform its image and policies, it stood a good chance of being overthrown from within.

The peaceful coup in October 1979 was accomplished by a moderate segment of the El Salvadoran Armed Forces (ESAF). The revolution was well planned. The leaders had the backing of the majority of the military, while General Romero's inner circle was helpless to intervene. It was dissatisfaction within ESAF that finally led to the change of government.

The coup triggered a round of political change that continued into the next decade. To make matters worse for the new coalition government, in 1980 radical groups and moderates opposing the government of El Salvador set aside their mutual differences to form the Revolutionary Democratic Front (FDR: Frente Democrático Revolucionario).

*Background*

This political coalition allied itself to the Faribundo Martí National Liberation Front (FMLN), combining five guerrilla groups into a loose alliance that eventually numbered an estimated 12,000 fighters.

The leaders of the coup sought to establish a junta following the historic model of Latin-American politics. They focused on sharing power, with key power centres, in an attempt to establish a unity of effort around the military's proclamation to institute reform objectives.

Without the ability to effectively establish its authority, the first junta disintegrated and was replaced by a second one in January 1980. Napoleon Duarte was chosen to head the new government, ultimately becoming the democratically elected president of El Salvador in May 1984. The Duarte government faced multiple problems.

US President Jimmy Carter meets with Salvadoran President Carlos Humberto Romero. (Photo White House staff)

Various opposition parties joined ranks with the FMLN in 1980, quickly becoming an extremely effective guerrilla organization. At this time, the ESAF had slightly over 15,000 soldiers, which, as anybody who has studied recent insurrections is aware, is inadequate to effectively confront a guerrilla force of at least 7,000, or roughly half as many as the defending force.

In October 1979, the three biggest problems in the ESAF included a shortage of equipment, lack of training, and most importantly, a lack of preparation to confront a united guerrilla force. In contrast, the Salvadoran armed forces that were tasked with countering this escalating insurgency were also their own worst enemy. Their continual abusive treatment and blatant human rights abuses of the citizens were seen as a form of 'business as usual'.

Death squads ran rampant, and although both sides undoubtedly used the most brutal means to achieve their objectives, including so-called death squads, the ESAF seemed to be more closely associated with this practice. The bodies of victims who had been murdered by these assassination groups would almost routinely show up each morning at two well-known locations: El Playón, the lunar lava fields outside of San Salvador, and Puerta del Diablo, a tourist centre in the mountains. Reporters, MilGroup (the United States Military Advisory

Group in El Salvador) personnel, and tourists could follow vultures to find the locations of these killing fields.

Half a century of oppressive military rule, the basic denial of human rights to the working class, and a concentrated system of land tenure combined during the late 1970s to foment the crisis that led to the civil war.

On the regional level, the ascendancy of the Marxist Sandinista regime in neighbouring Nicaragua aggravated an already unstable political environment in El Salvador. If these trends were not turned around, either internally by the new government or externally in cooperation with the United States, the FMLN, by co-opting the peasant population of the country, stood a good chance of ousting the government. To keep this from happening, both the Carter and Reagan administrations acted decisively. Washington not only supported the Salvadoran government, but also 'declared war' on the spread of communism in Central America, and indirectly on any country supporting communist expansion.

US embassy in San Salvador. (Photo Jesse Michael Nix)

Cuba's Fidel Castro and Nicaragua's Daniel Ortega met often during the war. (Photo RIA Novosti)

President Jimmy Carter concluded that the Sandinista government posed a threat to the stability of Central America and to United States interests in the region. After President Ronald Reagan took office in 1981, he not only adopted Carter's view, but then went still further. He considered the situation in El Salvador to be a target of opportunity for the Soviet Union in their continued attempt to spread communism in Central America. Unless the Soviets were stopped, Reagan argued, they would continue to try to expand their influence throughout the Americas.

Clearly, the Reagan Administration could not and would not allow that to happen. It made the decision to halt the advance of Marxism on the battlefields of El Salvador. Deane Hinton, United States ambassador to El Salvador from 1982–3, stated: 'When I went down there, the mission given to me by the government, the Secretary, and to some extent directly from the President, was to make sure that the guerrillas and Communists didn't take over El Salvador.'

# 2. A DIRTY, DISTANT WAR

I went to El Salvador with former Vietnam veteran, Captain Bob MacKenzie. It was a good choice as he had been a captain in the Rhodesian Special Air Service, SAS, even though he had a crook arm from a war wound that saw him invalided out of the US army. That was some years before he fought with Renamo guerrillas in Mozambique. Bob had also worked as a mercenary in the Balkan war where he trained Serbs in some of the subtler esoterica of insurgency warfare.

Bob MacKenzie's career as a 'gun-for-hire' did not end well. This affable, always-smiling, totally unflappable American freebooter, became the first white officer for some decades to head a West African fighting group, the Sierra Leone Commando Unit, SLCU. That ended within a comparatively short time when, on 24 February 1995, he was killed in an ambush by bandits of the Revolutionary United Front, RUF.

The conflict in El Salvador was a very different kind of war compared to most other guerrilla struggles. There were several reasons, the first being that both the Soviet Union and Cuba had a marked influence on its outcome. As we have already seen, Washington backed the other side, not only politically, but with a limited number of men (restricted to fifty-five serving soldiers by an act of Congress), machines, hardware, and whatever else was needed to keep San Salvador from becoming a Comintern clone.

A lot of people died in that terrible conflict that totally ravaged this tiny Central American state, but in the end, with solid United States and Latin-American support, a peace was negotiated. Against all odds, it survived the strains of some of the most convoluted and conflicting interests in the hemisphere. Critics called it a loveless, superficially 'arranged' marriage, but it finally worked. At least the shooting stopped, and more recently El Salvador sent over 3,000 of its troops to fight in Iraq.

The country's civil war took an atrocious toll, not only in terms of lives lost, but in an economy that was stripped of just about everything. After almost a decade of fighting, there were about 75,000 people dead and several million exiles, more than a million of them in the United States.

## A Dirty, Distant War

FMLN guerrillas. (Photo Linda Hess Miller)

El Salvador, it would seem, had always been under some sort of tyranny or oppressive role. By the time the author arrived in the mid-1980s, the country reflected hope and desperation in equal parts, always the ultimate recipe for revolt.

Its real misfortune of course, like that of Nicaragua next door, was to become a pawn on the great international chess board that reached as far as Angola, Aden, Tanzania and what can be observed today in Afghanistan. Eventually, Russia lost the game, not on the battlefield, but with the collapse of the Soviet Union at home.

In Central America, it all began as a domestic quarrel. In 1980, a group of landowners and coffee traders in El Salvador launched a military coup. They were supported by the police, the judiciary and the army. The idea that motivated the putsch was to perpetuate the old system of political control that one still today sees in many Third World countries that keeps the establishment rich and the rest of the people poor. Those growling masses who opposed the plotters, including many churchmen, were murdered, exiled or driven into rebellion. It was hideous, and therefore small wonder then that the Russians and their Cuban surrogates, perhaps quite justifiably in hindsight, armed the oppressed and took over the revolution, for that was what it was.

Such was the leaden symmetry of the Cold War, that it was that old warrior-leader Ronald Reagan who chose El Salvador as the place to 'draw the line' against communist encroachment in the Americas. In the end, it cost the US taxpayer six billion dollars, not much by today's standards when Iraq cost the American taxpayer hundreds of times as much, but in those not-so-long-ago times, a sizeable sum.

Washington's tactics included a grand strategy to sap the rebels' support by fostering democracy, land reform and civil rights. To some extent these moves, while moderating the homicidal propensities of the army, did not altogether stop them. The Rand Corporation, in a report to the US Defense Department, calculated that in 1981 alone, the army and its agents murdered 10,000 people. The new political dispensation in San Salvador reduced that figure to about 100 almost ten years later.

In many ways, the civil war in El Salvador resembled a hundred civil wars before. It was mostly the unarmed, the dispossessed and despised civilian mass that seemed always to be at the receiving end. They suffered first from a succession of corrupt and brutal governments, then later from a guerrilla force that kicked off their campaign with laudable intentions to begin with, but very soon became no less murderous and oppressive.

To the grandly named Farabundo Martí National Liberation Front, you were either for the revolution or you were against it. There was absolutely nothing

## A Dirty, Distant War

in between 'only black and white and no greys,' as one American advisor tried to explain it to me one evening after a diplomatic function.

The war in El Salvador made one lasting impression on the author. Nowhere else had he seen so many young men who had been crippled by landmines. Even the guerrilla struggles in Rhodesia and Angola were nowhere near as bad. Yet few of the correspondents ever mentioned that dark aspect of war when they left this Central American crucible of violence – it was almost as if those casualties did not exist. Yet, they were there for all of us to see.

In El Salvador, the prosthetically endowed were a rarity. There was simply no money for such 'luxuries', as the authorities described it fairly early on, although with time, things did change. Throughout the war, most of the national budget was devoured by hostilities that not only started at the edge of the capital but, with assassinations of prominent people, sometimes well inside it. The mines that had crippled these men were small anti-personnel devices, or 'APs' in the terminology, usually buried a few inches in the dirt near a path or stream that might be frequented by the enemy. Many were little round Russian-made PMN-2s, which weighed less than half a pound and could fit comfortably in the palm of a man's hand.

Then there was the TMA-3 or TM-57 anti-tank mines (the one Yugoslav, the other Soviet). These were bigger, heavier and more difficult to hump in any quantity across mountains, but the guerrillas did exactly that, and these devices took their toll as well.

The conventional wisdom about such things in this kind of insurgency is that it is better to maim a man than to kill him. A wounded comrade needs three or four others to tend to him and carry him to safety or to the nearest clinic. This means more manpower tied down when soldiers in the field should be doing their job. Still more effort and money would be spent treating this casualty.

Sadly though, ultimately anti-personnel mines caused many more casualties within the civilian population, especially in indigent rural areas than they did among the combatants. Children were the worst affected.

FMLN guerrilla near Suchitoto, 1984.
(Photo Gary Mark Smith)

*Above*: FMLN guerrillas. (Photo Ralph de Leon)

*Left*: A female FMLN guerrilla. (Photo FMLN)

# 3. FIRST IMPRESSIONS

The city of San Salvador is not a grand place in the tradition of Rio or Havana. It snuggles untidily between two rows of hills in the Valle de las Hamacas, the Valley of the Hammocks. When I was there, it seemed to be the only city in Latin America with no colonial buildings left intact.

Once it had been the capital of the United Provinces of Central America, when there had been plenty of fine old buildings erected by the successors to the Conquistadores. All of them were destroyed in a succession of earthquakes and floods during the past few centuries. Of course, there are plenty of tall buildings, but San Salvador, clearly, was no Manhattan. Most of these stunted, unattractive glass and concrete blocks looked like they'd been plopped down at random in the expectation of another catastrophe, which is perhaps understandable because the country boasts more active volcanoes than most.

San Salvador in the 1980s. (Photo Sammiethedeadrat)

## El Salvador

A rural scene with an army APC as a backdrop. (Photo Susan Meiselas)

beans and chillies and shared a few beers with the *campesinos* as they stood guard at the edge of their settlements. Elsewhere there were attacks and ambushes. People were dying.

We never felt personally endangered in any way, whether at base or on patrol, but the fact is that this was one guerrilla war in which the rebels remained undefeated on the battlefield, until the Americans stepped in with their comprehensive MilGroup aid program. That turned this war on its head.

Whatever the ultimate consequences, it would have been a scoop for the FMLN insurgents to have been able to kill or wound one of us *extranjeros*, a propaganda victory that would have been valuable, especially if the link to *Soldier of Fortune* was exposed. The 'mercenary' syndrome was never distant in our minds, especially since Bob Brown was financing some of his own people to train irregular units. The government knew this, and probably also quietly encouraged it. Consequently, the army and the air force took good care of us.

All the guys were 'carrying' and none of us took chances. Most the men who arrived with Colonel Brown also had the advantage of having had good combat experience.

*First Impressions*

Dana Drenkowski has some good memories of the war. *Soldier of Fortune* magazine leased two large suites at the Sheraton Hotel over a period of several years, knocking out the walls between the two suites to make a huge central chamber with couches and foldaway beds and a pair of bedrooms on either side. He comments:

> One side, as is the case with all hotel rooms, was exterior facing, making both the room and us vulnerable to attacks by satchel charges or rocket-propelled grenade onslaughts, the RPG-7 being the weapon of choice among most guerrillas. As a result, the main room was sandbagged up to window height, with still more sandbags in other strategic areas, including the bathroom.
> 
> Hotel maids were never allowed into our 'retreat'; we did our own housekeeping and the place was kept pretty clean. At the same time, precautions were justified: two US AID officials had been assassinated in the hotel coffee shop by enemy hit teams not long before we got there. And, of course, we were well aware that we were on their lists.

Brown's not-so-little hotel complex was the base of ops for several foreign military types (with no official connection to their governments) who passed through San Salvador between missions in the bush. And Drenkowski wasn't the only one getting past, legally, the US Congress-imposed fifty-five-man limit. He adds:

> How many more irregular fighters there were, I'll never know, but I was aware that, like me, all were embedded with the El Salvador military forces and went out regularly on combat missions, in addition to training their troops.
> 
> I was friends with probably half or more through my jobs elsewhere, and most of the rest were connected to Bob Brown and his magazine in some way, as was I. One was quite famous in our rather arcane circles. He was an extremely competent pistoleer, a former Rhodesian SAS operator and US paratrooper, and a veteran of many other wars.
> 
> When not in the jungle fighting Gs, he organized and taught weapons-defence courses to fellow military and certain well-placed civilians who believed they should know how to shoot to protect themselves and their families. He knew exactly what he was doing and was highly regarded by all.

*El Salvador*

A Salvadoran marine receives instruction from his US counterpart. (Photo Alan B. Owens)

Drenkowski was advised that whatever he learned and saw in El Salvador would be reported to two sources: US Intelligence and Congress, the latter behind closed doors and in secret. As he explained, 'this requirement to report would be an expanded part of my chapter, to include those closed-door briefings.' Drenkowski continues:

> I'm not sure how much of that story I can tell, as there were some interesting occurrences involved. For instance, I spoke in those sessions to a joint House/Senate armed services committee. Everyone was present but for one certain extremely radical Democrat congressman whose seniority should have made him the chair of that committee.
>
> However, when the prior Dem chair departed and that congressman should have taken over by virtue of his seniority, the Democratic leadership quickly substituted another senior congressman from within its ranks, in what was described to me as an unprecedented violation of tradition and Democratic house rules. That substitute Dem Congressman took over as chair of the committee, but he was never to be allowed to see Top Secret documents, period.

According to Drenkowski, there were good reasons for this anomaly:

> That dubious Congressman on the far left met monthly with the head of the World Peace and Freedom Organization (based in Stockholm, Sweden), who was a reputed lieutenant colonel in the KGB. They met in the congressman's office, which was off limits to all wiretapping or bugging ever since the FBI entrapped several congressmen in their offices in the earlier AbScam sting operation.[1]
>
> This monthly meeting was reported by some investigative journalists as the monthly meetings between an agent (either direct or an agent of influence) and his controller – a spy meeting with his boss. That Congressman was well known for his anti-American statements and standpoints, and there is a lot more I can tell about him, but this is neither the time nor the place.

In the world beyond the Sheraton Hotel, where most of us spent some of our time when in the capital, the daily events of war were close enough for every one of us to be aware of what was going on in the jungles, coffee plantations and farmlands beyond.

Once, while being ferried in a Huey towards a hillside village to the west of the Conchagua volcano, we were fired on from the ground, but the pilot could not see where it was coming from. On a second pass, tracers could be spotted rising from a thick clump of tall trees.

Later that day, the El Salvador air force tried a trick of their own. They sent in as a decoy one of their little two-seater Bell scout helicopters, the intention being to draw fire, and then have the Huey 'Mikes', which were circling nearby, rake the area with their Gatlings. A few thousand rounds in five- or eight-second bursts would do the necessary, was the way one American airforce officer attached to a local squadron briefed us. While it sounded simple enough, it wasn't. Such attacks were precision-guided, needing a bit of luck as well.

At other times, it seemed that the guerrillas were conspiring against us personally. Perhaps they were. They would wait until after we had left an area before hitting a target. They certainly knew we were there because some of their leaflets mentioned us.

What worried us, as journalists most, was to be mistaken for an American, with a good chance of a bomb chucked through the window of a bar or

*El Salvador*

A government soldier directs his squad. (Photo Gervasio Sánchez)

restaurant where we were eating, or to be killed while eating lunch in a little bistro in a backstreet in San Miguel.

I did not appreciate how dangerous San Miguel was until I began to take photos in the centre of the town on the morning of my third day there. I'd gone out alone and wandered down some side streets looking for opportunities. What did surprise me was that there were almost no soldiers around. Within minutes, while focusing on the twin steeples of the cathedral, two Jeeps screeched to a halt right alongside where I was standing. Out tumbled a squad of soldiers who fanned out around the courtyard. The officer in charge, wearing a bullet-proof jacket, ran towards me, seized me by the arm, and, bundling me into one of their vehicles, told me that the place was very dangerous.

Back at the base, the camp commandant had apparently received a call from one of his informers in town that I had been wandering about on a private jaunt. I'd been through San Miguel often enough by then for just about

*First Impressions*

Entrance to the 3rd Infantry Brigade, San Miguel. (Photo LI1324)

everybody in this frontline town to know that I was working from the Arce Battalion base with the rest of Bob's team.

Obviously annoyed, the commander told me that the rebels had shot at (and missed) an English couple working as missionaries in a government school one evening a few weeks before. It was obviously a case of mistaken identity, for the rebels did not intentionally kill those 'helping the cause'. But then, he said, it is those mistakes that they worry about.

Battalion headquarters at San Miguel, our base, was a fort in the old tradition. The walls, four metres high, were painted in a gaudy combination of brown, green and yellow dazzle. The corners rose into French Foreign Legion machicolations in a Disneyland effect that could not have been intentional as it had been built over a century ago to defend the eastern part of the country when insurrection was endemic. Over the main gate was a black sign with yellow lettering BATALLON DE INFANTERIA DE REACCION IMMEDIATA.

The name Arce (pronounced Arcey) commemorated one of the fathers of the nation, General Manuel José Arce. It was a tough, efficient special unit that had seen its share of action in the war and had not disgraced itself.

Security was tight. A strongly held sandbagged guard post about fifty yards from the main entrance commanded access to the two roads leading directly to the fort and, invariably, the guards looked as if they expected trouble. It was an exposed position. They were occasionally sniped at, although that did not stop mothers and sisters from hanging about waiting for a chance to visit their menfolk.

Once inside the great doors, things were a bit more relaxed. Soldiers not on duty lounged about in T-shirts and shorts, playing board games or *futbol* on the soccer field at the back. Much of the rest of the area was dominated by cavernous warehouses, which also served as barracks. Officers were billeted more comfortably near the battalion HQ, which was set somewhat apart. All windows in the outer walls were covered with wire netting, though occasionally someone would throw a grenade over the walls.

I was surprised at how rough the barracks were, crowded and none too clean. The men slept in long rows of stacked iron beds, three, four, even five high. There was little space for stowing of uniforms or equipment, the troops making little heaps of their belongings along the walls. Anything of value was carried in pouches on their belts.

We ate with the troops – it was execrable. But even in the officers' mess, the cuisine was deadly dull, again mostly beans. The colonel, as we were aware by then, preferred to eat out.

It was there too that we spotted several soldiers who had lost limbs. Most of these casualties had a foot missing, from mines. When asked why they were not sent home as they were no longer of any use, we were told that they were local boys who would be singled out when they went home as having fought against the guerrillas, and face execution. They were free to leave whenever they wished, but preferred to remain in the security that their former unit offered them.

The battalion had a combat record of which to be proud. Placed as it was in one of the most contested zones of the war, with Nicaragua along the way across the bay, there was a lively *esprit de corps*. Every evening at stand-to, the men would lustily sing the regimental chorus. It was all stirring stuff and could be very clearly heard by everybody in town.

As the war developed, government forces became more obtrusive with their defences. (Photo Al J. Venter)

Every one of these young soldiers, few of whom had reached their age of majority, willingly went about his duties. That could not always be said for some of the other units we visited. If one were to judge by the large number of large Arce crests about – a yellow dagger on green surrounded by red – one knew exactly where their loyalties lay. *El Ejercito Vivirá Mientras Viva La República* was the battle cry – the army will live while the republic lives. It too stood in bold yellow letters above the main gate.

# 4. COVERING THE WAR

Arriving after dark in any country where there is a war, presents conditions that you're usually warned about beforehand. For one, you simply do not wear camouflage when you travel. Second, you never move about in airports with an empty pistol holster on your belt. Some of our group had both, even though we were being met by American military aid personnel who were already working there, including Harry Claflin who was in-country, having volunteered for an assignment with the El Salvador Airborne Battalion, Reconnaissance Platoon.

We had barely entered the concourse of the El Salvador international airport before it became clear that we were scheduled for a grilling by the authorities. A bunch of officials viewed us warily and, I suppose, they good reason to because we certainly weren't your usual run-of-the-mill tourists, even if there were any coming to the country in wartime.

Whilst being questioned about whether the author's boots were for mountain climbing, Colonel Robert K. Brown interjected in Spanish that they were there to see action against guerrillas. He had been with Fidel Castro in the Sierra Maestros during the final stages of his revolution, but that was before the Cuban leader had begun to refer to his closest friends as *camaradas*.

It was to be expected that the airport functionary that had taken a liking to me would view this very vocal bunch of gringos with distrust, especially since Donovan had warned us earlier not to take anything for granted. He made the point, quite valid as it transpired, that while America supplied El Salvador with all manner of assets, the severest critics of El Salvador's civil war were also Americans.

Another customs man found a pair of Vietnam combat boots in Foley's baggage. This caused the arrival of a new lot of officials. Brown then identified himself and produced a letter from the El Salvador minister of defence.

The officials went into a huddle, made some calls to their superiors and, in an hour, we had become local heroes. That done, and after another few beers, we set out for San Salvador in a decrepit old bus along a deserted road.

One of the reasons for all this kerfuffle, apparently, was the discovery, some time before, of combat gear in the luggage of a Scandinavian mercenary on

*Covering the War*

These freshly minted government troops are straight out of school. (Photo Al J. Venter)

*El Salvador*

his way to join the FMLN guerrillas based in Nicaragua. His travel agent had unwisely booked him through El Salvador when he should have gone to Managua. We never did discover his fate.

San Salvador, the capital, lies about fifty-five kilometres from the airport. There were several army roadblocks and, to my surprise, precious few lights along the way. Guerrilla ambushes, we had been warned, had been frequent. Not long before we got there, three American nuns and a lay worker had been killed on that same road by a rebel group. It was an accident, they told a newspaperman in Managua afterwards: they had believed their victims were military. Anyway, they declared, they shouldn't have been travelling that road at night.

Vietnam veteran Harry Claflin, who had been in El Salvador for some years by the time we got there, training El Salvador special forces, eventually saved the day for us. He had brought along to the airport half a dozen M16 rifles and enough ammunition to start a war. With these passed around, the men settled themselves comfortably in the bus at seats by open windows, each one of them hoping desperately for an ambush that never came.

I had long intended to go to El Salvador. The only man that I knew that could get me and my cameraman into that war was Colonel Robert K. Brown, owner and publisher of *Soldier of Fortune* magazine. For the trip to El Salvador, we went to Brown's house in Boulder, Colorado in November 1985. There we were joined by MacKenzie and John Donovan, an extremely powerful bald chap with a neck like a professional wrestler, which, I gathered afterwards, he had also tried his hand at. Donovan was a major in the US reserves.

Brown, our host, and Paul Foley, who had spent twelve years in the French Foreign Legion, headed the team: Foley, in his fifties, was a tall, sinewy man who thought nothing of a thirty-mile hike through the mountains as a preparation for a Saturday night's thrash. Most times he was quiet and reserved, but things would change when he had had a few. Then he could spring into action in a moment, whether on patrol or in one of the bawdy bordellos that the men liked to frequent in the seedier parts of town.

Having followed his progress over the years (he was at MacKenzie's memorial service in San Diego), I doubt whether Foley would ever have been comfortable in anything but a uniform.

Paul Foley was decorated for bravery when he jumped with the Legion into Kolwezi in the Congo at the time of the Katangese invasion. As he tells it, it

Former Rhodesian SAS operator, Bob MacKenzie. (Photo Al J. Venter)

was an attack by rebels that left hundreds of Belgians, including many women and children, dead. Les Paras whipped them in forty-eight hours. Those few rebels still alive fled back to Angola. As is the custom in these uprisings, very few prisoners survived.

All ten of us flew first to Houston, Texas, where we had been booked on an airline that I had never heard of before: TACA. To me, that was not at all reassuring, considering that we would be arriving at El Salvador in the dark. I had been told by one of the men that, in recent years, there had been several incidents involving commercial airlines in the mountains that surround the country's main international airport, especially during bad weather. It was raining when we left.

Our route included a stop in Belize, a former British colony that, at the time, was regularly used for tropical-warfare exercises by elite British units such as the SAS and SBS. In those days, Belize was constantly under threat of attack from Guatemala, its bigger and more belligerent neighbour, which always regarded the little stretch of mangrove swamp and jungle fringing the Gulf of Mexico as its own.

*El Salvador*

*Left*: Propaganda and psychological warfare were undertaken by both sides.

*Below*: A Salvadoran family home defence unit with US weapons. (Photo Government of El Salvador)

# 5. MORE AMERICAN INVOLVEMENT

Towards the end of the decade, the Americans became much more involved in interception work along the coast, especially off La Unión. US Marines were brought across to man island-based electronic observation sites in the Gulf of Fonseca. SEAL teams were also drafted in. These crack navy specialists, the equivalent of Britain's Special Boat Service, would probe Nicaraguan defences, which, at the time, was totally in conflict with American and international law. The United States was not at war with that country and, in any event, the US constitution didn't allow for such things. That, however, did not seem to bother President Reagan. In those days, the American defence establishment could do such things and get away with it. Most times, anyway.

At one stage, Washington even sanctioned the mining of the Nicaraguan port of Corinto, which had become a major FMLN staging post for the struggle

Salvadoran patrol boat, La Unión. (Photo Racael L. Leslie)

in the neighbouring country. The United States Navy tank-landing ship (LST), the USS *Sphinx*, was detached for this purpose, causing much damage.

All these forces coordinated their activities under the auspices of Claflin's MilGroup, run from a discreet San Salvador headquarters by one of those shadowy figures of the Cold War, John Waghelstein.

For all that, the mid-1980s was a time of upheaval for El Salvador. The country was going through a period of transition, from possibly the worst army in Latin America to one of the best, in which Waghelstein was to play a pivotal role. Other Americans who saw service there remember the epoch as a period of confusion. Still more regarded the dedication of some Americans involved as foolhardy. There were dubious missions carried out into rebel territory that should not have worked, but they did. Had they happened anywhere else in the world, it might have been regarded as suicidal.

In Central America, while the war went on, Ilopango Air Force Base on the outskirts of San Salvador enjoyed the kind of mystique that had previously enveloped places like Vietnam's Da Nang and, possibly, Ondangwa in Namibia. All had been operational air force bases.

There were strange things that happened at Ilopango: midnight flights, helicopter airlifts involving large numbers of troops who could usually be seen quite clearly sitting at the open doors of Huey 'Mikes', clutching automatic weapons; and the occasional ambulance, sirens wailing, would mysteriously arrive and depart.

Part of the problem in El Salvador, as hostilities dragged on, was that both sides became steadily more desperate to make some kind of mark on the events before them. At the same time, Washington was openly reviled by the rebels. Any Americans in El Salvador at the time, whatever their politics, were identified with the ruling military junta. Few were tourists or journalists. Most were closely shorn members of Washington's Outer Beltway establishment. The majority were attached to military missions or acted as diplomatic 'observers'.

We had remarkably free rein at the Ilopango Air Force Base, considering that it was the nerve centre of the war. Decisions were made by the chiefs of staff at military headquarters in the city, but it was at Ilopango that these orders were put into effect as nothing in this war happened without close air support.

It was strange indeed that Alwyn Kumst and I were permitted to wander about the base with our cameras and take whatever footage we pleased, which would be most unusual in any other war these days. The authorities didn't

FAS Cessna O-2 Skymaster, Ilopango. (Photo Al J. Venter)

even ask to see what Kumst had been filming. Since they had only Brown's word for it, everything we shot could have been handed over to the guerrillas for a fee and nobody would have been any the wiser.

To one side of Ilopango, there were several helicopter squadrons, most of them Huey 'Mike' assault helicopters, some armed with multi-barrelled 7.62mm guns. (The UH-1M – thus 'Mike' – was a utility helicopter converted from the US Army UH-1C to an attack helicopter during the Vietnam era, since replaced by the AH-1 Cobra. The UH-1M was upgraded from the UH-1C model with a more powerful Lycoming T53-L-13B 1400 shp engine.) This was the Escuadrón de Helicópteros. In our time, they flew raw – no Kevlar floor matting to protect either the crews or anything vital round the engines or hydraulics. Later, specially designed and mounted engine armour was added as well as AN/ALQ 144 infra-red jammers to deflect SAM missiles.

We would fly out in single-aircraft sorties, which didn't excite me. In the Angolan War, all sorties into the unknown were always two-ship operations, sometimes more. Who would get us out if we went down? That was my first question. The second was, if we went out on our own with no support chopper, who would know where we'd gone down? When the El Salvador air force started losing more aircraft to ground fire, they adopted that practice as well.

Then came a couple of squadrons of A-37 light-support jet fighters. They were trainers, really, but gave excellent service, often swooping in low and dropping ordnance where needed. I knew that they used napalm, but the authorities denied it. It was uncivilized, they said. The insurgents in the mountains, who were at the receiving end, would have agreed.

It was the Huey 'Mikes' that brought real carnage. As the war progressed, their firepower was augmented by multiple-rocket launchers mounted over twin 7.62mm guns. The men on the ground would send up a flare or a smoke marker over an enemy position, and these choppers would do the rest.

We could travel as we pleased from Ilopango Air Force Base with any aircraft flying at the time, and we often did. Kumst hitched a ride on one of the machines that went on a strafing run. As his ears were unprotected, we couldn't speak to him for a week afterwards. I was sure that he must have suffered some permanent damage. Still, he argued, it wasn't macho to use protection of any kind among the boys.

Travelling about with the 'Mikes' had its moments, especially in the eastern mountains. There was one particularly well-defended hilltop position near the Honduran frontier that the government liked to attack. The rebels, however, were well entrenched in a defensive system that included caves and trenches, from where they could beat off one onslaught after the other.

Operational shot of an FAS Cessna A-37 Dragonfly. (Photo Martin Hornliman)

*More American Involvement*

After a Huey had been lost to ground fire there, some of Brown's troupe suggested that we go out on one of the operations then being planned. It would be a strike in depth to unseat the enemy, was the terminology used. Brown, however, would have none of it.

In Salvador, I was to discover, helicopter warfare was very different from elsewhere. The same machines were employed, but this was a different kind of jungle terrain – much of it mountainous – and a much more resilient adversary.

For one, these Hueys would fly at an altitude that the Americans liked to call 'avoidance radius', a planning figure used to determine the distance that an aircraft should keep from a particular air defence weapon or system to avoid effective fire. It sounded complicated. Yet, looking back, it seemed that we must have presented easy targets. At 4,000ft, we were certainly well within range of any SAM-7s that we knew the guerrillas had acquired from Moscow.

We were also quite capable of getting hit by heavy machine guns such as the Russian-made 12.7mm DshK or the 14.5mm KPV, both of which the FMLN had plenty. Also, even though the weaponry was hauled in on foot, they never appeared to be short of ammunition. They even brought in some multi-barrelled ZSUs of the kind that had often awed me in Beirut and elsewhere in the Middle East in the past.

Still, while the guerrilla gunners didn't appear to be all that accurate, they chipped away steadily at the resources of the Fuerza Aerea. The losses were never made public. One only heard about incidents on the grapevine, usually when a Huey or some other helicopter was shot down. Waghelstein's MilGroup knew exactly what was up, and had come down, but they weren't telling us hacks.

By the time we had arrived 1986, it was clear that most El Salvador aircrews were under strain. That was when Washington stepped in and brought in the 'Pigs': American air-crews working in rotation from Honduras in forty-five-day tours of duty. The name came from them referring to themselves as 'Danger Pigs'. They called the Hueys pigs too, because by then those choppers were out of date. They would have preferred the same Black Hawks that their colleagues sported in Honduras, where a less intensive guerrilla war was underway.

The Americans came into El Salvador as B Company, 4th Battalion, 228th Aviation Regiment in July 1987, but their home base for the duration was Soto Cano Air Base in Honduras. Door-gunners were drawn from the 193rd. They did tours of six months. While in San Salvador, this very committed

*El Salvador*

Side gunner on an FAS 'Huey' gunship. (Photo Al J. Venter)

group of individuals lived in a safe house, which, some say, was the third-best-defended structure in the capital. The crew was discreetly taken to work at Ilopango and back home again in a van with tinted windows.

All these Americans followed complicated procedures that soon became part of the daily routine. Targets were jointly assessed by MilGroup and the chiefs of staff. The crew would then assemble on the night before an assignment to discuss routes, intelligence reports and other relevant information. Each crew used a complex assessment matrix to project the level of danger likely to be experienced, whatever that might be.

Some South African pilots who had been at Ilopango (among them Dick Paxton who also flew helicopter gunships in Sri Lanka) said it was like having a photograph in front of you of somebody's lungs who had died of cancer while you were enjoying a cigarette. You knew there was danger. There was always danger, but you soon learned to live with it, he told me nonchalantly.

Several aircraft were shot down over enemy lines in this war, both helicopters and fixed-wing machines. The crews, if they survived the crash, and there were a few, were not treated kindly. In one attack, long after we had departed, ground fire brought down a Huey 'Mike' outside the village of La Estancia about twelve miles north of San Miguel, the same area where we were later, with a ground patrol, to visit former coffee plantations.

The senior pilot, Chief Warrant Officer Dan Scott, was taking Lieutenant Colonel David Pickett, officer commanding the 4th Battalion, 228th Aviation Regiment, back to his headquarters in Honduras. He had been on a staff visit to El Salvador. For a shortcut, they had flown from San Miguel towards San Francisco Gotera, before tacking towards the north-east. That way, he reckoned, they would reduce flying time and slip inside the established 'Green Three' route into Honduras that led direct to Soto Cano.

The twin M60s, with which the Hueys were customarily armed, were strapped to the floor of the machine because, officially, American aircrews could not fly with mounted guns. For the duration of that trip, therefore, they were inoperable. Again, it seems, the Americans were the only ones playing by the rules. The fact that the helicopter traversed a hotly contested region of conflict did not appear to matter, plus, in any event, nobody told the guerrillas that the helicopter was not armed. So they shot it down anyway.

As the war dragged on, the FMLN suffered large numbers of casualties. In the first six months of 1985, the El Salvador armed forces were responsible for about 3,200 insurgent losses, out of about 8,000–9,000. That figure includes more than 1,500 of the enemy who had surrendered. In the same period, government forces lost 810 men killed, wounded or missing.

When the war began, the air force of El Salvador, or FAS (Fuerza Aérea Salvadoreña), barely existed, even on paper. By 1983, it had twenty operational helicopters, and less than two years later that had increased to sixty. With that number of aircraft, pilots had to come from elsewhere, which was when quite a few foreign aviators entered the picture, including a bunch from South Africa.

This kind of escalation must have put enormous pressure on the guerrilla command. The attrition rate to their forces would have been unacceptable. Like it or not, there came a time when the FMLN would have to answer to the families of the dead. This was, after all, a people's war. It therefore came as no surprise that Nidia Diaz, a seasoned guerrilla commander with years in the field, when captured by an FAS helicopter hunter-squadron (a combined air/special ground forces operation), was found with a document showing that, already then, the rebel command had abandoned all hope of an outright military victory. The gist of it was that a negotiated peace was the only way – some cadres were beginning to say so publicly. Still, it took almost seven more years of fighting before that happened.

The El Salvador Air Force badge.

Central America. (Image CIA)

Salvadoran girl alongside a mural at her school, Sonsonate, El Salvador. (Photo Aaron Smith)

*Above*: While in the east, the author operated with the crack Arce Battalion. (Photo Al J. Venter)

*Below*: El Salvador army patrol moves through an urban area in eastern El Salvador. (Photo Al J. Venter)

*Above*: An FAS Huey circles prior to landing. (Photo Al J. Venter)

*Below*: Approaching the eastern seaboard in a Huey. (Photo Al J. Venter)

Insignia of the El Salvador military.

Section leader of the army unit that the author accompanied. (Photo Al J. Venter)

*Above and below*: Salvadoran army special reaction units parade at their launch, April 2016. (Photo Office of the President of El Salvador)

US and Salvadoran naval personnel on a US Navy rigid-hull inflatable. (Photo Kim Williams)

A Salvadoran sailor on a US Navy boat departing from the HSV-2 *Swift*. (Photo Kim Williams)

During the civil war, the FAS operated MD 500s, used as gunships and armed with 7.62 mm miniguns and rockets. Three were lost to SA-7 missiles in 1989 and 1990. This later version of the Policia is based at Ilopango International. (Photo aeroprints.com)

Salvadoran Policia Huey at Ilopango International. (Photo aeroprints.com)

Monument to the Heroes of 1811, Plaza Libertad, San Salvador. (Photo Efegé)

Monument to the Divine Saviour of the World, located on Plaza El Salvador del Mundo, San Salvador. (Photo Alexbonilla2013)

The 'permanent offensive' by the government compelled the rebels to reduce their forces from battalion-sized units to sections of anything from five to a dozen men. The transmogrification became more marked when their objectives started to become more economic than military. What followed was an intense round of sabotage. Bridges and power lines were blown down and assassinations increased, together with ambushes and agitation among students and labour movements.

As we flew between Ilopango and San Salvador, we could observe the upshot of some of these tactics. In one area, close to the capital, there were long lines of power pylons that had been neatly knocked over with an explosive charge at each concrete base. We also flew over numerous bridges that had been blown. At one stage, we even put down where a huge bridge straddling the Trans-American Highway had been destroyed. Due to the danger of mines, we were not allowed to move about in the area.

By then, about a third of the population was unemployed. Despite military successes, things were deteriorating economically. That happens when so much of the army is tied up in guarding static assets such as bridges, electric plants, dams and the like. As a result, more ordinary people were voting with their feet and taking their money with them. The untenable situation was not sustainable. The rebels, despite heavy losses, remained active until the end. They showed remarkable versatility and an utter ruthlessness of purpose throughout.

There is a school of thought that considers the FMLN, in its day, to have been one of the most effective unconventional armies of the time, for the simple reason that, when they fought there were no inhibitions. They waged their war in the age-old traditional manner of using every means at their disposal to destroy the enemy.

On recon operations, when a sector was chosen, each unit had to keep a very accurate account of everything that happened in their area. If they encountered houses or villages, they kept records of every person living there: male, female, dress, where they worked, and if of military age, where they went day or night. The result was that we eventually had a complete record of the activities of everybody in their respective sectors.

The bottom line was that if the Gs were using one of the houses in an area that we had already covered, we would know about it. There were no indoor toilet facilities, so everybody had an outhouse. If we wanted to make a capture, we'd keep a record of when the person went to use the crapper at night, and then send in a team to take him. And as the Gs never took their guns with them to take a crap, we would just wait until they were on the seat, open the door, tape his mouth shut, put a sack over his head, and head off into the jungle with him. Most times, if we believed the captive had information, we'd call for an extraction by chopper, so that the individual could be taken back to Ilopango for questioning.

The people in those villages or houses would never be aware of what had happened.

As Claflin explained, these was some of the operations he helped to organize and run.

He later added something about the people selected for the GOE, which did not take long to become one of the country's elite units.

For a start, he explained, those hoping to make selection had to be able to read and write and have at least two years of combat behind them. They would also need to have a real reason to go after the guerrillas, such as having had family members murdered by them or injustices suffered at their hands, which, surprisingly, was quite commonplace.

On the physical side, I noticed, while on patrol with members of an Arce unit out east while with Bob MacKenzie, that the average government soldier was not the finest physical specimen around. I suggested that since they were mostly peasant stock, many had probably been malnourished when young. When asked how he handled that, Claflin explained:

> Most did not have a lot of upper-body strength, but could walk all day with a 50-pound pack on their back. We worked out a PT program for them and

Entrance to the main Arce base. (Photo Al J. Venter)

they were given a high-protein diet. Also, their pay was twice what a normal Salvadorian soldier got, and with all that and the pressures we put them under, we never had a single member of the unit who quit.

We did lose people from accidents and there were a couple of guys that killed themselves, though we never did find out why. Both men had been in the GOE for over five years. We also had one man killed by a policeman while on leave over Christmas in 1985. He was at a local bar in his home town at the time and the local cop knew him. Being GOE, he was carrying a pistol and the cop accused him of stealing it since he was not an officer. The guy told the cop to go fuck himself, and with that, the cop shot and killed him.

The basic problem there was that our guys would not broadcast that they were members of an elite combat group: it might ultimately play out badly with their families back home if the Gs ever came around, which they did, of course. Two weeks later the cop got into his car and it blew up.

I was back home in the States for Christmas and by the time I got back, I was brought in for a talk about what had taken place, the suggestion being that the dead man's GOE buddies had murdered the cop in retaliation for

FAS Douglas C-47 on static display, Ilopango. (Photo aeroprints.com)

killing one of their sergeants. If they did do so, and they probably did, they were very smart about it. The entire team – all 27 of them – was on an operation at the time on the Honduran border. Also, they could prove it from the chopper manifest. I even subsequently asked them about it and they all denied knowing anything about the killing. At the end of the day, we all knew who was responsible. We just couldn't prove it, so the official record stated that cop was killed by the guerrillas.

It says a lot that the Grupo de Operaciones Especiales was the only unit that the FMLN demanded be disbanded during the peace talks in 1993. That eventually happened – fully disbanded, with everybody then being drafted into the El Salvadoran Special Forces that did not leave the military. All the records of those who served within GOE teams, as well as every after-action report (as well as my own), were destroyed after the war.

# 7. MILITARY ADVISORY GROUP

One of the most important documents to emerge from this Central American conflict was written by Major Paul P. Cale, titled 'The United States Military Advisory Group in El Salvador, 1979–1992'. His introduction is concise: 'The US Military Advisory Group in El Salvador helped an emerging democratic nation combat a communist-supported insurgent threat.'

Effectively, this diverse bunch of military professionals assisted in transforming the El Salvador Armed Forces (ESAF) into a professional military force, going in immediately after the Carter administration made the decision to support the San Salvador government with economic and military assistance.

Salvadoran marines undergoing weapons training from US Marine Corps personnel. (Photo Alan B. Owens)

As Major Cale states, in addition to the US Marine Corps guards and military personnel stationed at the American Embassy, the first advisors flew into the country in November 1979, a month after the *coup d'état* that ended the Romero administration.

Cale continues with his dissertation on the build-up of the Military Advisory Group at length, starting with the premise that the American press compared the sending of military advisors to El Salvador with the opening stages of the military build-up in Vietnam in the early 1960s.

He goes on:

> During the 1980s, the Reagan and Bush administrations had to convince the American public that the conflict in El Salvador would not become 'another Vietnam'. The American support of the government of Salvador with military personnel and financial aid, was prescribed as the 'Nixon Doctrine' [and] human rights violations within El Salvador, on both sides, and the threat of a 'Vietnam-type mission creep' remained fixed on American headlines throughout the 1980s.

Early in 1980, the Salvadoran government faced two difficult and conflicting problems. First, they had to maintain the financial aid they were receiving from the United States by convincing the American people with the idea that they were fighting a communist insurgency. Second, they had to fight the insurgency with the only doctrine they knew: the use of brutal repression against their own citizens.

Human-rights advocates berated the Salvadoran government for allowing the death squads to exist. At that time, an incident occurred that served to escalate the already bloody conflict. El Salvador always had a strong Roman Catholic identity. Most Salvadorans in the 1980s were Roman Catholic and church rituals permeated the nation's culture and society. On 24 March 1980, the Archbishop of San Salvador, Oscar Romero – no relation to the former president – was murdered at his altar during mass, sparking the onset of open warfare in El Salvador.

The Catholic church in El Salvador was seen by the government, and specifically the ESAF, as being openly supported by opposition parties. In the early 1980s, the most important intellectual force in the country was the Jesuit University, La Universidad Centro Americana José Simeón Cañas, UCA.

In San Salvador, the Jesuits were ignored by local scholars because of the university's close association with the left. Near the end of the conflict, in November 1989, six Jesuit priests, as well as a housekeeper and her daughter, were murdered by military-sponsored death squads.

By November 1980, guerrilla bands became more organized and took their message to the people. Documentation obtained by the Salvadoran government showed that guerrillas had brought 600 tons of weapons into El Salvador. The information also indicated that they could equip approximately 15,000 soldiers. The FMLN proclaimed that a final offensive would take place in January 1981.

Although a final military victory was not achieved, the organizational structure of the FMLN, and its ability to conduct effective military resistance, indicated that the guerrillas were well supported and supplied from external sources.

On 7 January 1981, an operational and planning assistance team (OPAT) arrived to aid in protecting the harvest from the guerrillas. By the end of the Carter administration, nineteen US military advisors had been deployed to El Salvador. When President Reagan was sworn into office, his administration began explaining to the American public the significance of the threat to United States national interests posed by the communist insurgency in El Salvador. This White House public affairs effort allowed the president to dramatically increase both the amount of financial aid and the number of military advisors sent to that country.

A white paper published in February 1981 offered definitive proof that the Soviet Union, Cuba, and their allies had been sponsoring the insurgent movement in El Salvador. It stated that this was another case of indirect armed aggression aimed at a small, Third World country by Communist powers acting through Cuba.

The support received by the insurgents was intended to help them overthrow the government of El Salvador. With the Soviet Union sponsoring one side and the United States sponsoring the other, El Salvador became the latest battleground for the 'super powers' to settle their ideological differences.

On 17 February 1981, Secretary of State Alexander Haig briefed members of NATO on the nature of the problem facing the United States in El Salvador:

> Our most urgent objective is to stop the large flow of arms through Nicaragua into El Salvador. We consider what is happening is part of the global

Communist campaign coordinated by Havana and Moscow to support the Marxist guerrillas in El Salvador.

The policy implications are already clear: First, the US government supports and will continue to support the present government in El Salvador. We intend to work with that government with the objective of achieving social justice and stability in that strife-torn country.

Second, the United States government is convinced that neither stability nor social justice in El Salvador is possible if Communist subversion continues.

Third, we will not remain passive in the face of this Communist challenge, a systematic, well-financed, sophisticated effort to impose a Communist regime in Central America.

While the United States sent financial aid, and deployed military advisors to El Salvador, the American Congress debated the issue. Congress's biggest fear was that 'mission creep' would set in and the American military presence would slowly transform itself into a repeat of the disaster faced in Vietnam.

Anti-El Salvador Civil War protest, Chicago, 1989. (Photo Linda Hess Miller)

By March 1981, the number of military advisors assigned to the MilGroup was steadily increasing. The increase of advisors deployed to El Salvador was not coordinated with the Salvadoran government. The author believes that the administration coordinated directly with the El Salvadoran armed forces and not with the Salvadoran government, due to a belief in the White House that the ESAF was actually running the country, and not the members of the junta who were struggling to establish their legitimacy.

After the democratic election of President Duarte in May 1984, the legitimacy of the Salvadoran government had been established. By the mid-1980s, the leadership of the Salvadoran armed forces clearly recognized its subservience to a freely elected civilian government.

On 3 March 1981, President Reagan addressed the American people in an interview with Walter Cronkite. The definition of 'military advisor', as well as any parallels between Vietnam and the insurgency in El Salvador, was answered by the president:

> You used the term military advisors. You know, there's a sort of a technicality there. You could say they are advisors in that they're training, but when it's used as advisor, that means military men who go in and accompany the forces into combat, advise on strategy and tactics. We have no one of that kind. We're sending and have sent teams down there to train. They do not accompany them into combat. They train recruits in the garrison area. And as a matter of fact, we have such training teams in more than thirty countries today, and we have always done that; the officers of the military in friendly countries and in our neighbouring countries have come to our service schools – West Point, Annapolis, and so forth. So I don't see any parallel at all.

The Reagan administration, in March 1981, accepted a compromise with Congress that set a fifty-five-man limit on the number of US advisors deployed to El Salvador. The dual MilGroup mission of reshaping the Salvadoran armed forces into a professional military that respected human rights and in rapidly increasing ESAFs size, was thought by MilGroup to require more advisors than the agreed limit. The limit was a political compromise that kept aid flowing into El Salvador. The fifty-five-man limit may have been the best thing that happened to the ESAF during the 1980s. The limited number of advisors forced the Salvadoran armed forces to accomplish the military mission on the ground after the American advisors had trained them.

The initial group of military advisors deployed throughout the different military regions of El Salvador was appalled by what they saw, and the lawlessness that the country's citizens faced. The countryside resembled a state of anarchy, with roving bands of soldiers terrorizing the population. The condition in El Salvador looked less like a war zone than it did a general collapse of civilization. Immediate attention would have to be placed upon increasing the professionalism of the Salvadoran armed forces by the American advisors. Training would be the vehicle to accomplish that mission.

This first contingent of fifty-six US military personnel deployed to El Salvador by the end of March 1981 were broken down into the following functional areas:

> Six MilGroup staff at the US Embassy, increased from four;
> five Mobile Training Teams (MTT), working in the MilGroup, for administrative, logistics, and command purposes for the increased personnel;
> six Naval Training Teams (NTT), to assist the Salvadoran navy in improving its capability to interdict seaborne infiltration of arms destined for the leftist guerrillas;
> a total of fourteen helicopter training and maintenance personnel;
> five men in each of fifteen small-unit training teams to provide garrison training for the Salvadorans new quick-reaction force;
> two OPAT teams of five men each, basically to aid each of El Salvador's five regional commands in planning specific operations.

Included in the initial group were army special forces soldiers who had been specifically trained for that type of operation. American 'Green Beret' special forces soldiers were also in El Salvador to help train Salvadoran military personnel in communications, intelligence, logistics, and in other skills designed to improve their capabilities to interdict infiltration and to rapidly respond to terrorist attacks.

Counterinsurgency training was the primary mission given to the Green Berets assigned to El Salvador. Due to their extensive knowledge in many

Plaza de Armas training area in La Unión, El Salvador, 2011. (Photo US Department of Defense)

types of combat skills, these troops found themselves providing training to the Salvadoran armed forces on a wide range of subjects.

The Reagan administration's acceptance of the fifty-five-man limit on American advisors in El Salvador seemed at times as only a way of satisfying Congress. Several times during the 1980s the American military presence in El Salvador exceeded the agreed-upon limit.

By the end of 1984, there were over a hundred American military personnel in El Salvador. Three years later, that number exceeded a hundred and fifty. The actual fifty-five-man limit related to the number of military advisors assigned to a one-year tour in El Salvador. In addition, numerous Special Forces 'A' Teams of twelve men each were deployed to El Salvador to conduct unilateral training throughout the country. These teams remained for between six and twelve weeks before returning to their unit of assignment in either the United States or Panama.

Through the spring of 1981, the State Department continued to downplay the comparison of El Salvador to Vietnam by citing statistics. Their publicly stated intention was to reduce the number of US military advisors in El Salvador by the summer of 1981, during which period the advisors were prohibited from accompanying Salvadoran armed forces on any type of patrol.

The Department of State also mentioned that the United States had 525,000 military members in Vietnam in 1968 conducting combat operations. For every military training advisor the US had in El Salvador, there were 10,000 combat personnel assigned at the peak of the American commitment in Vietnam.

Financial aid given to the government of El Salvador continued to rise throughout the early to mid-1980s. The 1982 fiscal year request brought the total US military assistance to El Salvador, since 1980, to $62 million, almost four times that which had been provided over the previous twenty-year period. Even with the vast amount of aid that was flowing into the country however, by the summer of 1981, it appeared likely that the guerrilla movement, led by the FMLN, was on its way to success. The American advisory effort would need time to make its presence felt in military victories. How long the government of El Salvador and its armed forces could hold off the FMLN was impossible to predict.

Human rights abuses, primarily conducted by militarily supported death squads, almost caused a cessation of American support to El Salvador.

In October 1981, the US Senate established conditions for continued US aid to El Salvador. President Reagan had to certify twice a year that the Salvadoran government was making marked progress toward controlling the ESAF and their known death-squad activity and other human rights violations. The American democratic form of government was founded upon the pillars of freedom, liberty and justice for all. Communism in contrast, as portrayed by the Soviet Union, was looked upon as 'the evil empire'. In this regard, it should be remembered that Lieutenant William Calley Jr and his court martial for leading the My Lai massacre was only a little over a decade old.

America could not be associated with, or openly supportive of, a government that supported violations of human rights. The United States Congress would not allow the moral high ground to be taken away from the United States by death squads operating in El Salvador. Congress ensured this did not happen by using the only means at their disposal, their constitutional control over American financial resources.

Evidence collected on the battlefield in 1982 confirmed that FMLN insurgents were backed by communist states throughout the world and weapons captured by the ESAF were traced back to the US involvement in Vietnam. After the Ilopango raid in 1982, captured demolition material was traced to Czechoslovakia. East German, Bulgarian and Hungarian equipment was also recovered after several military operations.

The Salvadoran armed forces and the MilGroup advisors believed that military equipment was being brought into El Salvador with the help of the Sandinista regime in Nicaragua.

President Reagan took every opportunity to get his message of the significance of the situation in El Salvador across to the American people. In March 1983, in a speech to the National Association of Manufacturers, Reagan stated, 'If the FMLN were to win, El Salvador will join Cuba and

Mayor Osmar Ovidio Cruz hands keys to the city of La Unión to Captain Tom Negus, CO of the hospital ship USNS *Comfort*, during Operation Continuing Promise, a four-month humanitarian and civic assistance mission to seven countries in Latin America and the Caribbean, 2009. (Photo Ashley Garcia)

Nicaragua as a base for spreading fresh violence to Guatemala, Honduras, even Costa Rica.'

Political members of the opposition in El Salvador were keenly aware that whether they would achieve their goals in El Salvador was directly affected by how well President Reagan and his administration could get their message across to the American people. Reagan claimed that if American military aid to the Salvadoran government was terminated, the regime would collapse and El Salvador would fall into the hands of communists. And all said and done the 'great communicator' did in fact get his message across, and with the fifty-five-man military advisory detachment, limited United States presence in El Salvador passed muster of Congress and the American people.

One of the few operational coffee farms during the war. (Photo Al J. Venter)

# 8. CENTRAL AMERICAN CRISIS

The civil war raged on in El Salvador, fuelled by US aid to the Salvadoran military and lasting longer than anybody had expected – a dozen years in all, almost twice as long as the Americans fought in Vietnam. As with all conflicts, both sides reacted with vigour, brutality and, at the end of it, at least 75,000 people lost their lives in military actions, political killings and bombings. On the more conventional side, and in retrospect, some of the actions provide a fascinating insight to a modern guerrilla struggle.

The guerrillas hit the naval base at La Unión on the Gulf of Fonseca along the Pacific Coast of El Salvador some months before we arrived. They killed dozens of young conscripts for the loss of only a handful of their own.

It was a signal victory. The guerrilla fighters entered the base sometime after midnight. They had evidently reconnoitred it very carefully over a long period and they knew exactly what obstacles had to be overcome. First, they cut the throats of the guards, and then, without firing a shot, they were among the barrack buildings, throwing grenades into open windows before anyone was even aware of their presence. The raid caused a great stir throughout the country as many families had lost their sons.

A year later, in March 1987, a similar raid was carried out on the headquarters of the 4th Brigade at El Paraiso. Altogether twenty soldiers were killed, though there were reports doing the rounds while we were there, that the actual figure was something like seventy-five, possibly more.

An American instructor, Sergeant First Class Greg Fronius died while trying to rally a defence after the Salvadoran officers had abandoned their men. Guerrillas attempted to overrun the camp and kill everyone still alive, but they were not as successful as they might have been. Once over, enemy losses, said Claflin, were estimated to be around seventy. The real figure remains in dispute because the guerrillas always tried to take their dead and wounded with them. The idea was to avoid giving the enemy anything of a moral or propaganda advantage. Claflin explained that this kind of thing did not happen often, and that the outcome, as at La Unión, was seldom so critical.

*El Salvador*

SFC Gregory A. Fronius, training a Salvadoran soldier in marksmanship. Fronius was KIA on 31 March 1987 when rebels stormed a military base in El Paraiso, killing 43 government troops and Fronius, the first US military advisor to be killed.

Some people believed at the time that the attack on the naval base at La Unión might have been the turning point of the war. There were those who said that the FMLN had gained an irredeemable advantage, which was hardly true.

The reality was that the attack was admirably coordinated. Had losses been less, it might have been the kind of onslaught of which any guerrilla commander might have been proud. For the Salvadoran *Estado Mayor* (General Staff), it exposed a lack of order and discipline that was obviously extremely demoralizing and one of the reasons why the base at San Miguel was on such a high alert while we were there.

On the successes of the guerrillas, one of the more prominent 'neutral' commentators said that such attacks made it clear that government forces were getting little intelligence, or were possibly being fed batches of cleverly manipulated disinformation. He said on national radio that the nation was worried and that nobody in the country knew what was going to happen next. That comment labelled him a guerrilla 'fellow traveller'. His reports were subsequently viewed with a smothering of scepticism.

The truth was that the FMLN unit responsible for the La Unión raid had performed well. They had come undetected across the broad waterway between the two countries on the night of the attack in several small boats. Their radar images must have been minimal, helped by the fact that their weapons were already waiting for them in safe houses ashore. There was nothing untoward on their boats that might have alerted anybody on watch at the time.

But in the end, what the La Unión débâcle did do was to sharpen American resolve to take a more active part in the war. There were gaps in the defences of El Salvador that Washington proposed to plug. And effectively close them they did.

Many of the men with solid experience of other wars in Southeast Asia were sent to this Central American posting on government training missions. If they got into a few scraps during their duties, or accounted for a few Gs, then well and good. Each time it happened, the authorities would look in the other direction.

Pulling away from the Nicaraguan coast at speed. (Photo Al J. Venter)

*El Salvador*

That, however, did not apply to the media. American journalists made a thing of 'aid' people with weapons in their baggage arriving in El Salvador, much as they might have done about us had there been a journo around when we arrived. It would probably have been front-page news in all the major newspapers, especially if it could also be shown that one of our crowd had been a member of that ultra-exclusive little band of warriors known as USMILGP-EL, or in the lingo, US Military Group, El Salvador. We all talked quite simply about MilGroup, among whom American veterans attached to units of the El Salvador army did some outstanding work. As we know, with the benefit of hindsight, they helped to turn the war around.

Claflin, who spent two tours with US Marine Reconnaissance in I Corps when he ran that side of things along the Cambodian and Laotian borders with Vietnam, had his own views on what was going on in Central America. Harry's 'home from home' at Ilopango was nothing ostentatious, but it was secure. Though on a military air base, we were unlikely to take any 'incoming' so close to the capital. More importantly, it cost us nothing. When we didn't go out, we pulled out a few boxes of MREs – the ubiquitous, any-army 'meals ready to eat' – and all I had to do each morning was roll up my sleeping bag. He spoke with authority, having been brought to the country to coach the Grupo de Operaciones Especiales or, GOE, into an extremely effective counterinsurgency strike force.

> I worked with these local troops about a year and had gotten them up to speed. The stuff that I'd been doing with Recon Platoon in South East Asia came to the attention of quite a few people. In fact, the MilGroup took a lot of interest, so did the El Salvador chief of staff, which was probably why I was asked to put together a program to train a reconnaissance-type unit for the El Salvador army's 4th Brigade, an airborne unit.
>
> The idea at the time was to prepare the guys for special missions and they gave me a free hand. So, I could combine two programs that the Marine Corps had run in Vietnam, the Stingray Project and the Small Unit Action Forces Program. Stingray was run by Force Recon, and in its day was damn successful.
>
> Combining these two programs worked very well and so GOE went on to win its spurs. Other, similar GOE units followed and there's no doubt this project helped shorten the war.

You must remember that by 1983, when Washington first sent military advisors to help the El Salvador military, that country, like all Central American states at this time, was not prepared for war. Two years later, because of US help, the El Salvador military was up to the task of kicking the shit out of the enemy. What our fifty-five American advisors did was to take a Third World army and remould it into a modern fighting force. The success of the military, with which we were involved at a very basic level, was what led to what the media termed the Final Offensive in 1989. By then, FMLN guerrillas were getting desperate.

But their leaders, sitting comfortably way back behind the lines, most of them in Sandinista country anyway, wouldn't believe any of it. They couldn't accept that a tiny nation like El Salvador was fielding seasoned troops and getting results. This was a real blunder on the part of the FMLN, because they'd begun to believe their own bullshit.

They still held out the ideal of the people rising up with them and overthrowing the government. But it didn't happen, and it couldn't happen. Those same people on whom the guerrillas were counting had had a gutful of the FMLN. We ended up destroying the FMLN Military Wing and it was never to rise again.

As for the political wing, in the first presidential elections in which the FMLN could participate, the results said it all. However, because of the peace accords, they carried only one percent of the vote!

Today, many years after the fighting has stopped, El Salvador is by far the most modern of the Central American countries, and it is certainly the biggest friend we [the US] have in the entire region. It is worth mentioning that, for the all their setbacks, the guerrillas were still able to strike hard when they put their minds to it. This was very similar to the event in November 1989, that is still referred to as the Salvadoran 'Tet Offensive', a virtual re-enactment of the infamous combined Viet Cong and North Vietnamese forces' offensive in South Vietnam in 1968. It was certainly the FMLN's 'last-gasp' offensive and caught the San Salvador's military forces totally off guard.

What happened that memorable November day was a surprise offensive against military and civilian targets across the nation, especially in San Salvador, San Miguel and Santa Ana. The Ilopango air base where Claflin was holed up was almost overrun during the initial attack, the rebels threatening to

FMLN combatants, 1990. (Photo Linda Hess Miller)

destroy up to 80 per cent of Salvadoran air force assets. In bitter fighting over an extended period, the military incurred significant losses.

The guerrilla forces, however, not only failed to gain their objective, but they also sustained a heavy blow from which they would never recover. The engagement cost them 1,773 dead and 1,717 wounded. The air force also suffered one of its most unusual losses during this period of time, when an A-37B ground-support jet was hit in the cockpit area by a round from a Dragunov rifle. The co-pilot was killed, while the pilot ejected safely.

'The rebels remained active through the rest of 1989 and 1990, inflicting over 2,000 casualties on the Salvadoran armed forces and police per annum. We had forty helicopters shot down between 1988 and 1992,' Claflin said.

Several days into the author's own tour a few years earlier, at dawn one day, after we had been lifted out of a position in the hills north of San Miguel, our Huey pilot approached La Unión in the east of the country with circumspection.

He circled twice before landing, looking carefully about him as he did so. It wasn't that he was nervous, he assured us afterwards. In fact, he would have welcomed the chance to give his gunners something to shoot at.

He confided, however, that a small guerrilla unit had taken to firing at air force helicopters from the foothills every time the choppers approached and, he added, nobody could get a fix on their position to retaliate. We discovered afterwards that apparently the FMLN had somehow acquired a few SAM-7s.

That development was a good deal less disconcerting than it might have been twelve months before. From the air, we soon discovered that La Unión was not unlike the town we drove to the following day on our way to the naval base. It had once been a much bigger place, but the war had taken its toll. There were still coffee factories and warehouses on the outskirts, many of the suburbs were modern, extensive and very well laid out, but quite a few had been abandoned because of the conflict. With its distinctive red-tile roofs, friezes and Spanish architecture, before the war La Unión had been allowed plenty of space in which to grow. There was none of the congestion of San Miguel or some of the other towns in the region. On closer inspection, it was smaller than we had expected. It was also run down. The harbour, in contrast, was relatively new, or possibly, because of the war, it had been renovated and extended. Understandably, a bay opposite to where the guerrillas were operating from had a certain strategic value.

La Unión must have been a busy port before the hostilities. On our visit, there were only fishing boats and half a dozen naval craft. There were no small cargo boats, or even a tanker, like we saw at La Libertas farther to the west. Some of the smaller fighting boats were US Island-class patrol craft, a high-speed aluminium boat with a crew of fourteen. They had all been delivered to El Salvador after the attack on La Unión, which bore witness to the assertion about the war tending to change things, sometimes irrevocably.

Apart from soldiers on patrol, La Unión didn't look like a town at the business end of an increasingly acrimonious civil war. All the buildings in the business district, many with plate-glass windows, were still intact. Early each day, we could see that life seemed a lot slower than elsewhere in the country. At the same time, lots of things seemed to be happening: shops and cafés were opening, a postman was on his rounds, and a group of kindergarten children were being taken to school. Gradually, it became business as usual and, judging by the tone of its residents, the war might just as well have been in another country.

There were no formalities when we reached La Unión, either at the naval base or on the fast boat that was to take us out. At its masthead, it flew the flag

## El Salvador

of one of the Salvadoran navy's Reaction Force squadrons. The blue and white ensign on the mast bore the words *Dios, Union y Libertad* – God, Union and Freedom – across its broad, white horizontal stripe.

In a few minutes, we were on our way towards the other side of the gulf. The coast facing us, said the youthful captain, Byron Roberto-Rivas Alfonso Pinto, was Nicaragua. Having passed round his card – as protocol demanded – he suggested we call him Captain Bob. We now had three Bobs in our party: Bob Brown our unofficial 'leader', Bob MacKenzie and the skipper.

The thirty-metre patrol boat was immaculate. The crew had probably known we were coming and had prepared accordingly. There were two .50 Browning machine guns, one mounted fore and the other aft. It was good to see that the weapons were kept well greased. There were more automatic weapons mounted alongside the bridge. Aft, strapped down, was a five-metre rubber duck. The Zodiac performed a double function: as a lifeboat and for inshore patrols through shallow waters among the mangroves. The guerrillas got in everywhere, it seemed.

Salvadoran gunboat on patrol along the shores of the Gulf of Fonseca. (Photo Al J. Venter)

The crew was dressed in camouflage. There was nothing to distinguish sailors from soldiers – no formal whites anywhere. The heads below had also been scrubbed.

Life on board consisted almost solely of patrolling a fixed area out at sea. They would intercept and stop small boats and fishing smacks that crossed the bay, which was about fifty kilometres at its widest point. These civilian vessels were sometimes searched for weapons and illegal entrants and, if the crew was lucky, the captain said, they caught themselves an insurgent. He told us through an interpreter that they couldn't search every boat or arrest every suspect, but they knew that the guerrillas were bringing their people and weapons across. He added that the area was very active. They would sometimes, when they were sure, let one or two suspects pass to see where they led them. It was, however, a big complicated operation that needed a lot of men on the ground to follow the process through, Added to which, the guerrillas were not stupid either.

Captain Bob told us of something that had taken place a month before. He had stopped the same shallow-draught boat for the third time in as many weeks. It was always in the same area, and usually around mid-afternoon. They were even on nodding terms with the crew of two. Even though they had their lines out, Bob sensed something was wrong. There was nothing he could put his finger on, but he knew these hombres were up to something, but they were too clever for him.

He then did something that he hadn't before. They had some Pepsi on the boat and, offering them some, they came on board. They talked a little, about the weather, the fishing, the war, Nicaragua. Then, since it was getting late, the taller of the two men, a young fellow with sharp eyes and not much to say, offered Bob his hand – they had to be on their way, they told Bob.

The two men shook hands and, as the pair turned to go, Captain Bob realized that the hand he had grasped was not the calloused paw of a fisherman. The palms were soft, the grip flabby. This was no tarry sailor. Bob said he knew that he had them. Knowing he had to exercise care, they steamed on, but not too far away. In the meantime, they inspected several other boats, all the while keeping the suspects in sight. Bob said he then radioed headquarters to ask for a helicopter and a couple of marine commandos with diving gear.

An hour later, most of the support team was ready and waiting at La Unión, but the helicopter had to come from San Miguel, and that took a little longer.

*El Salvador*

The fishing boat hadn't moved, but with the light fading, Bob told me that he feared they would lose them. Fortunately, the sea was calm and there was no wind. Shortly afterwards, the familiar roar of a Huey could be heard. It approached from the shore, coming in directly towards them.

Bob told it to lower a winch, and in a minute, he was in the air. While the officer of the watch kept the boat in his sights, they made straight for it. Still in touch with the naval craft, their lookout said that the two men were hauling in their lines. They would have soon made off. They had only seconds to drop a marker, his own vessel following as fast as her 26 knots allowed.

The helicopter dropped its marker alongside the boat. The two men, now covered by a twin-barrelled 7.62mm machine gun, were ordered through a loudhailer to sit tight and wait for the navy. Two divers went into the drink, where they found a weapons cache wrapped in plastic bags attached to the fishing boat. The two on board had slipped the cable the moment they spotted

El Salvador's Pacific coast, sprinkled with a myriad of islands, ideal conditions for insurgents. (Photo Al J. Venter)

the inbound chopper. It was too late, however, as they hadn't reckoned on navy divers and the sea was barely six metres deep at that point.

This pair had been smuggling weapons into El Salvador from Nicaragua for months. On a previous occasion, when things appeared to go awry, they had simply jettisoned their cargo, allowing it to sink to the bottom without trace. It simply meant that they would go back to Nicaragua and get another consignment from the Sandinistas, who at that time, were getting an endless supply of weapons from Cuba.

The way the hardware was being shipped was interesting. Attached to the harness that held the loads, there were two small flotation bags that supported them just below the surface. In a cumbersome manner, the 'fishermen' could tow their loads ashore. If challenged, it was easy to turn over a bag and lose it. In those calm waters, they had ample warning. Visibility was invariably good, and when your engines weren't running, you could hear a man talking a mile away.

Senior FMNL commanders near the front. (Photo Wiki Archives PRTC)

# 9. NO MAN'S LAND

Several of us were taken by a Huey 'Mike' helicopter – a variation of the Huey Cobra – to one of the small settlements in the north of Morazán Department where we were to join a company of soldiers of the Arce Battalion. Our group included Bob MacKenzie, Paul Foley and a handful of others.

During the twenty-minute hop, we flew at 4,000ft, just high enough to avoid small-arms fire, although that placed us within what Claflin casually called the SAM-7 envelope. Envelope or not, it was the first time we'd been able to clearly examine the terrain in which we were working as it had been overcast before.

The mountains near San Miguel were almost all volcanic, though most were extinct. A few emitted intermittent puffs of smoke and, apparently, some of them had recently erupted. Every day slight tremors could be felt. The biggest one of all, Cacaguatique, sat dormant, but ominously brooding, near the coast, its peak perpetually in cloud or surrounded by sulphur fumes. Recent lava emissions were visible on its flanks.

Before we left, we had been told to prepare ourselves for a long haul. We would walk in column from dawn to dusk for three or four days, said MacKenzie, our route leading us into the same mountains that we were now flying over. The idea was for us to take only essentials along, together with enough water that we could manage – weight was a factor here. The army would supply the rest, MacKenzie disclosed, though, he warned it would be tough. He stressed the importance of taking our malaria tablets. The mosquitoes would devour us after dark, it was that bad. That said, we didn't have a mosquito net between us.

The Huey dropped us in a clearing in the forest that seemed to stretch all the way to the foothills. It was an unusual feature in a country where so much of the terrain seemed overgrown, some of it quite dense. It had once been a dairy farm, but the cattle were long gone. If the locals didn't eat them, the guerrillas did, suggested one of the soldiers who could manage a little English.

The pilot chose his LZ (landing zone) carefully, largely because one of the army units on the ground would provide cover. As in Vietnam, choppers in

Government soldier prior to going on patrol. (Photo Al J. Venter)

this war were most vulnerable when either in the flare for landing or when lifting off. Once down, he kept his machine on the ground only long enough for us to jump out. All the while, the door-gunners ranged their twin-barrelled 7.62s across the surrounding countryside.

First Lieutenant Carlos Alfredo Soto came forward to greet us, his light-brown face smudged with sweaty lines of camouflage paint, an M16 cradled in one arm while the other held the straps of a brown canvas map case.

He shook hands with each of us, welcoming everyone in turn. Youthful and energetic, he seemed genuinely pleased to have us with him and his English was the best yet.

Inviting us for coffee, Lieutenant Soto led the way to a small temporary base that had been set up in a clearing next to some old buildings. Most were covered in graffiti. One of the signs read, *Viva El 55 Aniversario de PCS*, commemorating the 55th anniversary of the Communist Party of El Salvador.

Half a dozen soldiers got up off their haunches to greet us. All of them were dressed in the same wavy green and brown camouflaged uniform and carried American automatic weapons. Their webbing was like that used by US forces in Vietnam, well suited to the tropics. An 81mm mortar tube was propped up against a tree trunk, but the bombs had been discreetly stowed a short distance away. Another officer was talking loudly into a field radio, a map spread out in the dirt before him.

The column that we had joined was larger than usual for this kind of upland patrol, about a hundred men in all. They were in constant touch with base and could have a 'Mike' over us in thirty minutes, if necessary.

Soto reckoned that he would welcome a contact, but he had to be wary of overextending his lines. The rebels sometimes like to attack with 300 or 400 men at a time, sometimes more. Although a government patrol had never yet been overwhelmed, it had been close. Whenever there were attacks, he assured us, there had been casualties.

FMLN guerrillas had overrun some army and naval bases in that fashion, attacking in depth, and always at night, he explained. I had heard of the disaster at the La Unión naval base, which was not far from where we had been put down. For that reason, and it is basic, he never allowed the men to extend beyond about 400 metres, thereby allowing for a rapid consolidation if the need arose. Air support was also available.

A soldier of the government patrol which the author accompanied. (Photo Al J. Venter)

*El Salvador*

Standard patrol routines in El Salvador's so-called hostile areas were rigorously applied. The men were taught never to bunch up or stand about in groups. There might be snipers about and they were sometimes very accurate, he warned. Any river or valley crossing was well reconnoitred beforehand. That usually involved a small scouting group establishing a bridgehead before the main body crossed.

Before we had left the barracks at San Miguel, the medical helicopter had brought in a soldier with a gaping wound in his thigh. The femur had been shattered and the right side of his body was riddled with splinters. He had already lost a lot of blood and, despite morphine, he was in great pain. They laid him on the stone floor of the medical room. It wasn't long before he was lying in a pool of his own blood. To our untrained eyes, it seemed that he would likely die. He had received the full force of a POM-Z anti-personnel mine that had been primed as a booby trap inside the door of a building within a couple of kilometres from where had landed. The man's officer was unsympathetic, saying that it was his own stupidity and he should have looked. They had been trained for that kind of thing.

Lieutenant Soto's men were a mixed bunch. Some carried obsolete 3.5-inch M20 bazookas, which were, nonetheless, useful weapons in this kind of country and good for retaliation when it mattered. While the rebels had the more versatile RPG-7, the men with the M20s were pleased with them, especially since they were made of aluminium and relatively light. Also, they could be dismantled when not in use. According to those who had originally produced this weapon, the maximum practical range was about 1,200 metres, though I have yet to see it hit anything at that distance.

There were also several M60 general-purpose machine guns, or GPMGs, spread along the length of the column. The men had faith in their American weapons, implicitly so it appeared, although with all that ammunition, there were some heavy loads to haul across mountains.

There was no doubt that there were guerrillas in the area. Soto graphically pointed out likely spots: a rare stretch of open ground at a tree line some distance away, a valley at the edge of our vision, and the mountains nearest us.

Lieutenant Soto was not the typical Central American conscript officer. Well educated and reflecting some of the attributes of the class he had been born into, he intended to become an architect when it was all over. He believed there was much to rebuild. He came from a wealthy family with land in the west, and

A well spread-out patrol of which the author was part. (Photo Al J. Venter)

had been to a private school in Mexico City where English was compulsory. After having been commissioned in the army, he completed a few months at an American military school on the east coast, but would not say where. It was not the sort of thing he would have liked the rebels to get to know about.

The FMLN, roughly estimated by Soto to be anything from 100 to 200, was obviously in the region in some strength, for when we passed through a little village in the afternoon and his men asked the usual questions, the *campesinos* were uncooperative. Some were aggressive. I was glad to get out of there.

Once we began walking it soon enough became a hard slog. I had taken the trouble to get myself into shape, but already by midday I felt done in. I had to compete with men half my age who had been nurtured up in these mountains – most were local boys.

We followed no determined route. Soto indicated to the north-east on his map and the man at point went off in that general direction. He wanted to reach a village before nightfall. He knew the people there and said it was relatively safe. Nothing, in that war, he stressed several times during the patrol, was secure. It was all a question of degree, he suggested, and, of course, preparedness. He had been instructed by the colonel back in San Miguel to see us through it all safely, so he was taking no chances.

So, we walked. Within three hours I had my first cramp. I sat down for a little while and said nothing because you don't want to let the side down. The undulating hills were the worst. We often had to climb out of gullies and ravines using our hands. There was also the heat, a hot-house clammy kind of humidity that made my clothes cling to my body within minutes, as if I had been doused with a bucket of warm water.

After an hour, I sought the first bit of shade ahead and lingered. Then one of the soldiers nudged me on. There was a note of urgency in their voices. The column marched at a brisk pace considering that it was supposed to be a 'casual' four-day patrol. Once they were on their way, the men increased the tempo. Taking pictures became difficult. I was beginning to lag, which worried me. That was when Foley came to my rescue and took my pack, the one that MacKenzie had offered to carry earlier. I declined the offer the first time, but didn't hesitate the second time round.

The author's patrol preparing to overnight at an abandoned school. (Photo Al J. Venter)

Every hour or so the column would halt, the men would light up a cigarette or throw themselves to the ground for a ten-minute break. We all sought shade, and even in those few minutes, some of the troops fell asleep. These youngsters had adapted well to a rigorous routine. Also, they made use of their opportunities.

When we reached the intended village late that afternoon, I was bushed. In about ninety minutes it would be dark. Lieutenant Soto dispersed his men carefully. Watches had been allotted before the squad had left San Miguel. The men knew their duties, but first he sent out several patrols to look for evidence of a possible enemy presence. Fresh tracks or food wrappers would be enough, Soto reckoned.

We 'slept' – for want of a better word – that night in a tiny hamlet of about twenty adobe and leaf-roofed buildings clustered round a small square. The village, one of the older settlements, lay on a gentle slope in the foothills, surrounded by some big trees that ran in a ragged line along what would have been the main track.

Pigs were everywhere. Since the rebels helped themselves, I was surprised that there were still so many around. Once there had been cattle, herds of them everywhere, but now there were very few left. That was a pity because, as in Africa, livestock is a moveable asset.

As it got dark, a marvellous aroma enveloped us all: wood smoke mixed with the scent of frangipani and bougainvillaea. The air was suddenly fresh and cool and clean. Elsewhere, someone was frying eggs. The village was poor and not at all clean, but I felt then, as I sat in the gathering dusk, that it would have been a great place for a few days' rest.

There were no more than sixty people in the place, all Indian or of mixed stock, which wasn't that unusual in a country where more than 90 per cent of the population was officially listed as *mestizo*. Before the war, in UN demographical studies, only one in a hundred Salvadorans had the dubious distinction of being classified 'white'. Until then, I'd supposed that only Israel and South Africa still categorized race. My first impression of these people was that while many looked a bit frail and emaciated, they would have done very well for themselves over many centuries without outside help. As rustic as they may have seemed to us interlopers, they appeared to be a good deal happier than their townsfolk *compadres*. They were a lot more content and possibly more sedate, in spite of the troubles all

## El Salvador

around them. They smiled when we arrived and they were still smiling when we left next morning.

I asked Soto how these local people managed. They were friendly to the army, yet, as I pointed out, this was 'bandit country'. Soto referred to the dwelling as a protected village in that they defend themselves. They ask for weapons and are given them. He explained that at first the rebels had tried to impose their own stamp of authority on these and other communities and there had been some fierce exchanges. Afterwards, when it seemed pointless to lose people for a cause that would ultimately be settled after the glorious victory anyway, the FMLN tended to avoid the place. Any *campesino* caught in the open or unarmed, however, was killed, always, as was explicitly stated when it happened, as an example to others. It was a price they had to pay, Soto reasoned.

The villagers were most vulnerable when they went into town, as they sometimes needed to do, possibly for medical, family or other reasons. The rebels would set up roadblocks, where they killed anybody they suspected of having dealt with government people. Soto added:

Break for an order group during the author's first four-day patrol. (Photo Al J. Venter)

It's all merciless. I can also be impersonal and cold blooded, which is what has really caused so many of these peasants to revolt. Talk to them yourself ... you'll quickly see that it's the system that the guerrillas are trying to impose on them that they really despise, one and all. That and the fact that they're all Christians.

The Church in El Salvador was often diametrically opposed to most things linked to government. It blamed the politicians for the war, and in some senses the priests were right, because it was greed that lay at its roots. That said, there is hardly a country in the western hemisphere that isn't battling some form or other of incipient corruption, though everybody was aware that El Salvador was probably more venal than most before hostilities started.

For this and other reasons, he reckoned, the Church was quite often sympathetic to both the revolution and the rebels, especially in some of the rural areas. The argument propounded went along the lines that the FMLN offered a better prospect of change. But nobody could reconcile the peasants' fundamental belief that Marxism was anti-Christ, not even the holy fathers. Some of the more passionate ideologists, the so-called 'worker priests' tried, but they never really succeeded. As Soto summed it up, to these simple, devout people, a communist is an atheist – end of story.

This came out while we sat talking after dark about the war. Often, we were joined by some of the NCOs and one or two officers, none of whom could speak much English, so Soto translated. There were probably guerrilla groups doing much the same thing in the mountains, almost within sight of us in the moonlight. The villagers that first night were as curious about us as we were about them. As an aside, I was rather disappointed to find that the troops were admirers of the American movie hero and cult figure Rambo. Even among the peasants of remotest South America, the junk-culture prevailed. It was ubiquitous, inescapable.

Next day we reached Santa Cruz, one of the three or four towns by that name in the region – all very confusing to us gringos. It was hard on us all from early on that day, first marching in a thick clinging mist that obscured everything, and later in rain and mud. It was miserable. I badly needed a shower. I also seemed to have been the only one to have been the focus of the mosquitoes, almost the whole night through.

After a brief stop for something to eat (beans again), we slowly climbed up a long path leading into another series of foothills. Twice, a single shot would ring out. The soldiers would hurry forward in that direction, but they couldn't see anything. The forest was too thick and response out of the question, reckoned Lieutenant Soto. At times, he said, if he had an idea of where the firing was coming from, he would have lobbed a few mortar bombs in that direction.

Ghosts walked by night in Santa Cruz. It had been abandoned for a year or two by the time we got there. There had once been a new administrative block and what appeared to be a fine two-level school, complete with playing fields and a boarding establishment for children from outlying districts. The buildings rather eerily echoed long-forgotten voices, or so I imagined. One of the walls out front had a huge hole in it, probably caused by a blast of some sort. It was creepy.

Santa Cruz had been heavily pasted by both sides as hostilities progressed. There was as much graffiti on the walls as pock-marked shell damage.

Derelict home, Morazán Department. (Photo Efrojas)

Artillery must have been used at some time or another, or was it possibly rocket fire from the 'Mikes'? A rebel had written across one of the walls of the main building foot-high words in red paint: *JOVEN INGRESA A LA ESCUELA MILITAR DEL FMLN* – ENTRY FOR YOUTH TO THE FMLN MILITARY SCHOOL. They had apparently used it as a training base. There were ammunition cases and cartridge shells just about everywhere. A Cuban party had even lodged there, another of the officers told us.

'Why did you allow them to hold onto the town for so long?' I asked Soto. 'Once you knew they had it, why didn't you take it again? Or at least try?'

'Ah,' he said. 'Thereby hangs a tale.'

Using his bush hat with a red band around it to shade his face against the sun, he pointed down the valley from which we had just emerged. 'You see where we came through. It's all tough country like that around here. The approaches too are very difficult. Lots of jungle ... the mountains behind us. Look,' he said, pointing.

A large range of hills did indeed undulate from one horizon to the other. There was only one road leading up from the floor of the valley and that was a good twelve to fifteen kilometres away. It wasn't metalled either, which, obviously, suggested landmines.

'The guerrillas have all the cover that they need. Anyway, when we arrived they just withdrew, pulled out, into the bush. It was a tactical retreat, a good communist procedure. They'd wait until we'd left, then they came back. Once we're gone from here, they'll return tomorrow again.'

'So why didn't you stay here; in force. Occupy the place permanently?'

'Because then they would fight like hell to drive us out. They did it two, three times. It became a point of honour. Then they shot down one of our helicopters and killed the three men in it. Although the crew survived the initial impact, they were executed on the spot. They displayed their bodies in a public place and wouldn't let anybody bury them,' he said.

It was a bad mistake, he suggested later, because such barbarism didn't go down at all well with the populace. That was when the military commanders in San Salvador had decided that enough was enough – if they cannot keep a permanent force occupying Santa Cruz, then the guerrillas would not use it either. Soto had warned earlier that none of us should wander about unaccompanied. Mines and IEDs were distributed about the dirt outside and he didn't know exactly where, he confided.

It was a pattern that had become common all over the country where regions or large towns were being contested by both sides. Santa Cruz, so near the Honduras border, which remained a conduit for men and arms for as long as the war went on, retained a high priority for both sides.

Steve Salisbury, an American journalist who had covered the war in those parts for several years, and was still around by the time the war ended, told me of another village that had been laid waste. That was Cinquera, which lay about eighty kilometres north of San Salvador. At a camp where she had gone to fetch money, he had met Maria Lydia Solis, a widow who not only lived through it all, but had survived. Cinquera was being defended by a squad of government troops. All the men and boys who could carry a rifle had been formed into a makeshift self-defence unit, but they had received little or no military training. Like much else in this war, it was all half-cocked.

The battle went on all night and the rebels entered the town in the morning. Although there had already been many casualties, including a dozen women and children besides the men who had been killed, the rebels lined up the survivors and shot them all. Only a handful of women and children were spared. Maria Solis was one of them. A substantial government force arrived a week later, offering no reason or excuse for the delay. Solis told the army commander that they had begged the soldiers not to kill them, but were told they must pay.

She told Salisbury that they had taken everything of value. FMLN cadres stayed for four days and then left. There were lots of horror stories afterwards. Since Cinquera was only an hour's drive from San Salvador, that sort of thing inevitably led to the question as to what was the army doing all that time?

Salisbury said that the worst was the wounded that they executed. The mayor and his secretary, who was Mrs Solis's husband, were both badly hurt. Señor Solis had stepped on a mine some weeks before, so he was already in a bad way, but no matter, they just dragged him outside and shot him in the head. The survivors abandoned Cinquera for good as soon as the army got there. It remained deserted until the end of the war, in large part because the few who knew it before were hardly eager to return and resuscitate the demons.

We didn't stay long in Santa Cruz either. For one, Soto wasn't happy. Also, he was worried about us. Radio intercepts had disclosed that the FMLN knew that a bunch of gringos – some of them with cameras – were with the column. Once before, he had been mortared while passing through. His platoon had

FMLN congress, 2015. (Photo President's Office, El Salvador)

lost a couple of men. He didn't need that to happen again. So we picked up our things and one more went on the march, if only to keep us all out of trouble.

In the old days, coffee had been the wealth of these uplands. There was much evidence of the old plantations, although most of the coffee bushes were going to seed. The graceful haciendas on the hillsides, offering magnificent views over the surrounding countryside, were still intact, although the owners had long since fled. None of the houses we passed was occupied, and from the detritus lying about, there was no question that the guerrillas had also called.

Whenever we came to an area that had formerly been habited, Soto warned us to be careful where we walked. He said that the rebels could see us coming from a long way off. Sometimes they had time to lay their mines and set booby traps, just like in Vietnam, he added. He insisted that his men search the place before we started filming or taking pictures, because he didn't need to be calling in any chopper to haul our corpses out of there. While MacKenzie and Foley were nonchalant, we civvies tried to follow instructions. We would follow one of the soldiers and, where possible, try to put our boots over his footprints. It wasn't always easy.

We could see by the settings and trappings of the estates that life in the old days must have been good. It had probably been a tasteful combination of opulence and a feudal tradition that went back centuries. Naturally, there had been servants galore, their quarters clustered in ordered array behind the main houses, as had always been the custom.

I asked Soto what would happen after the war. Would he and the other landowners go back to the old ways? He evaded the question; it was clearly embarrassing. But then he himself had been a member of the privileged class, so it was possibly understandable.

Of course, the peon soldiers who served under him knew it. But in countries other than communist, officers still command more respect if they were gentlemen. Even the Russians, having destroyed the old upper class, found it necessary to invent a new one.

Some of the farmhouses, though ransacked, were remarkably well preserved. One, on a hilltop that commanded views for thirty kilometres on a clear day, lay only a short hop by helicopter from San Miguel. It looked as if it had only recently been abandoned. In fact, it had standing been empty for years. We weren't allowed in because of booby traps, so we didn't argue. I heard afterwards that some government troops on another farm not too far down the road had been badly burnt by a phosphorus grenade set above a bathroom door. It was triggered by the light switch.

When the time came, getting us out of what had once been a minor paradise, was a bit of a dodgy exercise. Soto had long decided that it would have to be by helicopter.

On the morning of the fourth day, we had been warned that a chopper would arrive at a particular time. We were to wait on one of the concrete slabs where the coffee was once laid out to dry in the sun. Our cameraman was still filming, however, and he needed more time, so he took a while to make his way down to the improvised LZ. I could see that Soto was annoyed. The Huey, meanwhile, kept circling. The crew were in radio contact with the ground, in a hurry to get it over with. I knew that they felt exposed in those mountains. There had been choppers shot down. The Huey refused to land until we were all together. Then it became a hasty exit – a quick touchdown

An FAS UH-1H 'Huey' gunship. (Photo Miguel Castillo)

and an immediate lift-off. We were exposed for only a few crucial moments and, as luck, or fate, would have it, nothing happened that day.

I never did find out what happened to Lieutenant Soto afterwards, though a scandal soon enveloped San Miguel's colonel-in-charge. He was relieved of his command, but apparently it had nothing to do with military matters.

# 10. US MILITARY ASSISTANCE COMMAND

As we have seen, former Vietnam veteran Harry Claflin played a seminal role in creating a new breed of special forces elements within the El Salvador army. When he first arrived in the early 1980s, the special forces units were already established, on paper at any rate, but lacked any kind of expertise expected from an elite unit. As he comments, 'They were a raw, rum bunch ... it took a lot of effort to knock them into shape.' Below, in a succession of exchanges with the author, are some of his impressions from that period.

Claflin:

The American-backed Military Assistance Command was run by three commanders while I was there, but the one that had the most impact, and with whom I worked the most, was Colonel Jim Steele. He served from 1984 to 1991, which is a lengthy operational stretch in anybody's books.

A good commander and strategist, he did a great job. Looking back today, it is clear that he caused the guerrillas a lot of problems.

What he did achieve was all the more significant because he was restricted by a Democratic-run Congress to having only fifty-five American service personnel in El Salvador at any one time. Obviously, we found some discreet ways of effectively supplementing that total, but, as we have already seen, a handful of us were up against a guerrilla force of thousands.

On the US side, we had Mobile Training Teams that could stay in-country for eighty-nine days. They would then rotate out and return to their units the following day. Most of these were medical personnel and trainers at CEMFA, the National training centre for recruits at La Unión, not officially counted among the fifty-five listed OPAC Advisors.

As Claflin told me, the US Military did not ostensibly participate in combat operations in the war, certainly nothing that anybody back in DC could point a finger at.

Those men would only respond in the defence of bases where they were stationed when attacked. Their main job was to help build up the armed forces of El Salvador and, as we now know, they did an excellent job.

*US Military Assistance Command*

Senior Salvadoran and US officers meet, 2013. (Photo Hector Rene Membreno-Canales)

They had a significant influence on how the war was being fought and quickly moved the El Salvadorian military into the 20th century from a Third World military run by commanders who did not understand how to fight a new kind of war, a modern war.

It was all fundamental to start with, government troops emerging from training and going into action with good support from a variety of specialists, coupled with support from solid aviation assets as well as hearts and minds programs.

One of the problems we faced was that our relatively small teams on the ground – all seasoned veterans who had spent good time in places like Vietnam – were in sharp contrast to most of the enlisted advisors who did not have any combat time. They headed out to the conflict in Central America some years after Vietnam, so the majority weren't able to teach anything except what was in the military instruction manuals.

Essentially, that is why I was given the task of forming the GOE and making them fully operational, but, of course, totally separate from the Military Assistance Command. Also, I was very much my own boss in this newly established grouping, so I could go on combat operations with them.

Notably, while the MilGroup people gave me all the assistance I needed, they could not go operational, though obviously, some things happened there too.

Conditions were very different with the guerrillas, the FMLN fighters. According to reports that emerged during and after the civil war, the rebel Faribundo Martí National Liberation Front, in contrast, was a cover group for several splinter factions that fought among themselves – sometimes quite bitterly – for control of the political and military side of the war.

Their training, if you could call it that, was mostly from officers that had deserted the national army, quite often with help from the Sandinistas in Nicaragua. On top of which, each group of Gs went at it differently. Because of the lack of supplies there was very little weapons-training done.

Most of the hardware that reached the Gs was captured in 1979–80 by overrunning police and military bases, usually with assistance from sympathizers inside. In fact, until the Americans arrived in 1982, the average El Salvador soldier simply wore a uniform and had had very little training. That all changed once our people got into the war. But still, we were up against a numbers game.

Yet, as everybody discovered to their surprise, we soon learned how to make things happen. Despite President Carter limiting the number of US military advisors to fifty-five, things worked out alright in the end because our guys did such a good job.

According to Claflin, there were numerous other Americans involved in the war about which very little has been published. As he explained, you had, for instance, the CIA and the NSA as well as the Office of Naval Intelligence, or ONI. There were also army spooks as well as US Embassy personnel involved in the war in one way or another.

The Centro de Entrenamiento Militar de la Fuerza Armada, or as it was better known, CEMFA, was the military training centre of the El Salvador armed forces, which opened its doors in January 1984 near the city of La Unión. That was and still is the capital of La Unión, the easternmost department of El Salvador. According to the British publication *Jane's International Defence Review*, the exact location of the CEMFA was a place called Punta Ruca.

The facility, built under the supervision of US military advisors, became the Salvadoran military's principal basic-training base after the Honduran government stopped training Salvadoran troops at the Regional Military Training Centre in Honduras. With barracks capable of housing up to 2,000 recruits and 100 instructors, CEMFA remained operational throughout the war. It was also the base for a 250-member security battalion.

The place soon came to the attention of the enemy and was not impervious to attack. In fact, it went to the top of the guerrilla agenda for destruction because of the quality of work the facility offered. Consequently, in October 1985, an estimated 350 FMLN guerrillas attacked the CEMFA base, making it one of the largest assaults of the year, and which left forty government troops dead. The FMLN command stated at the time that the principal aim was to capture or kill any American training personnel they found there. But Salvadoran officials, while noting that there might have been up to a dozen US soldiers at the base during the assault, said that they had not taken part in the fighting.

The embassy in San Salvador put the number of Americans present at the time the base was hit at five. Claflin makes the point that, after being sent out from training to become operational with a unit, the average soldier in the El Salvador army received no further formal instruction in any military discipline. He adds:

> In any event, the American advisors did not train below company level, and most of the time battalion level. They were building both an army and an air force almost from scratch, and simply did not have the manpower or the time to train small units.
>
> The Airborne Battalion, in contrast, was the best trained of the units in Central America at the time, except for PRAUL, a secretive military force run by the CIA and the US Special Forces out of Ilopango Air Base.

When I raised the issue, he explained that PRAUL was quite similar to the PRU in Vietnam, also run by Langley:

> There was no non-commissioned officer corps in the El Salvador army to speak of. If you could read and write, they made you a sergeant. Weapons and equipment maintenance was simply non-existent. When I was assigned to the airborne battalion, they had twenty M60s, of which only five worked.

FMLN guerrilla, 1990. (Photo Linda Hess Miller)

Communications was even worse. The battalion had only five working PRC-77 radio sets, the rest were down.

I spent the first six months getting weapons and communications gear up and running. A major part of my problem was that there were no trained NCOs to keep an eye on the equipment, and to see that the work got done and the equipment properly maintained. Also, we knew from the start that the officers in charge of units were not going to check on equipment, a problem for almost the full decade that I was down there.

Guerrilla weapons consisted of FALs, G-3s, M16s, M1 carbines, M1919 .30-calibre Browning medium- and heavy-duty M60 machine guns. In contrast, I didn't spot any RPG-7s, AK-47 Kalashnikovs or a single SAM anti-aircraft missile until the 1989 offensive.

What we did discover was that the guerrilla army made its own mortars and IED's from quite a lot of crude, home-made stuff. All the mines I saw were electrically tripped. They also manufactured their own explosives, usually mixed with small amounts of Semtex that came from Cuba.

Of the five Hughes 500 choppers they got from us, only one was lost to ground fire. The rest went down because of pilot error and, at the end of it all, only one survived the war. The first 500 we lost happened when the pilot was chasing a G down a ravine and swung his tail into a tree – down it went.

The second was lost after the co-pilot had pulled the pin on a red smoke grenade. It dropped inside the cockpit of the 500 and they crashed. In the only one that was brought down by enemy fire, the pilot took a hit in his right hand and lost control of his machine which crashed.

By 1986, you started to see a modern army beginning to take shape in El Salvador. A year later you had a bunch of young officers who knew how to mix it in a modern war. That was when the Gs were starting to lose control, and which subsequently brought on the 1989 offensive, their last military action of any importance.

In 1985, I was given the task of forming a special operations group to go behind the enemy lines, and penetrate their units to find camps and supply dumps, and to kill as many of the Gs as they could find. So was born the GOE. Those small twenty-eight-man units did a great job and, in a lot of ways, forced the FMLN to the peace table.

*El Salvador*

Elements of the Salvadoran Cuscatlan Battalion training to react to IEDs. (Photo Daniel West)

Claflin played such a vital role in El Salvador's war, that his background warrants a look. He was born in the Mid-West and raised on a working cattle ranch. He was only 17 years old when he decided to try for the US Marine Corps. After boot camp, he went to radio telegraph school. There he volunteered for Force Reconnaissance, passed his entry tests and was sent, in turn, first to jump school, then scuba training, mountain climbing, reconnaissance, escape and evasion, jungle warfare and finally, off to Vietnam. Claflin continues:

> Almost two years of running reconnaissance and hunter-killer teams taught me my trade. Got shot up quite badly in August 1966 and spent eight months in hospital. Survived all that and was assigned as an instructor at the NCO School at Cherry Point, North Carolina.
>
> While there, I was offered a job with another branch of the government, whose initials I won't mention, and left the Corps. For the next thirty years, I was doing what I knew best and spent the final decade in El Salvador, before retiring in 1994. Now I live a quiet life with my wife, back in the Mid-West.

## US Military Assistance Command

Along the way, there were only three wives, having given up smoking, drinking and chasing wild women many years ago.

Following a question from the author about the nature of the missions he and his men conducted while in El Salvador, he told me about some of his strikes, quite interesting ventures:

It happened in an area along the border with Honduras where there is a small village that was in the area controlled by the FMLN. The Gs would recruit most of the time by forcing young men and girls to go with them. I had two troops in my unit, one of whom could easily have passed for a kid of about fifteen. The other looked to be about seventy. So, I sent them up to take care of the two guerrilla recruiters that were being a pain in the ass in this town.

They went in, in civilian clothes, of course, as granddad and grandson and went straight to a local bar that was being used by the Gs to recruit. Once there, they started to loudly complain how badly they were being treated by government forces in their area, and naturally both were soon recruited by these two thugs. They told my two guys to follow them, saying they were being taken for recruiting, so they headed out into the jungle. About a mile out of town, my boys pulled their pistols and killed them both – no formalities, it was a job done.

Another time, the team went to a G camp and posed as Gs from another area. After a week of spending time with this group, they got up early one morning and slit every throat in the camp. More than thirty Gs were killed.

Another mission was to find large guerrilla camps and report back to base so that we could get the air force to launch a strike on them. Very successful that one, too.

And that, basically, was how we worked, the kind of missions the GOE ran. After nine years, they became quite accomplished at it.

There was also a raid involving President Duarte's daughter who had been kidnapped by the guerrillas and didn't turn out quite like we hoped. We had received some good intelligence that she was being held in an enemy camp on top of Wasaphia, an old volcano of some size. Airborne was going to put in a blocking force at the bottom of this ridge where the camp was and my GOE team was assigned to make the assault on the camp – all twenty-eight of us.

The stage was set with airborne going in first and establishing their line. We followed in behind the half dozen assault choppers that were laying down suppressing fire in front of the camp in a bid to force the rebels to try to escape out the other side. The gunships kept their fire low so as not to hit the girl and obviously, there was a helluva lot of fireworks.

We could see Gs running about 200 metres ahead of us as we unloaded off the UH-1D troop carriers. It wasn't easy because the grass was about three metres tall, something we didn't realize until we started to go in. I landed on top of a huge rock and rolled off onto my radio operator. Fortunately, we weren't hurt, so moments later we started off towards the camp, with the gunships overhead keeping up a steady rain of fire until we were well inside the camp.

That's when we discovered that the place was deserted. No one was there. All the Gs had hot-footed it out the opposite side. We started going through the camp and found that it was a lot bigger than we had originally been briefed. Looked everywhere, but couldn't find the girl. Either they had taken her with them, or she hadn't been there in the first place.

As we got to the far end of the camp, the Gs suddenly emerged from the undergrowth and hit the Airborne Battalion. Then the shit really started. Once the guerrillas realized that no fire was coming at them from their camp, they headed back up the hill in our direction. Meantime, the airborne guys remained close on their tails.

Obviously, we could see from where we were what was happening, which was when I decided that it was perhaps time for us to move on. We were now taking fire from the advancing Gs and from the Airborne Battalion chasing them. I called in for a pick-up at our original drop-off point and it was one tough race to get back to the LZ.

We were picked up, but it was close, and as soon as we cleared the tree line, the attack choppers let loose at the camp to provide covering fire for the Hueys taking us out.

Claflin has vivid recall of what took place, because he was at Ilopango when it all went down.

As far as the raid on the G camp goes, we all got out with our hides intact and, personally, I don't believe she had ever left San Salvador. I'm convinced that she was helping the FMLN. Couldn't prove it at the time, but after she had been released, after supposedly spending a year of captivity in the mountains, she sure looked a picture of health and vitality.

Interestingly, Duarte had traded five captured senior FMLN commanders for his daughter, an action that almost caused a revolt among senior-ranking officers in the El Salvador army. Had it not been for the air force refusing to go along with the attempted coup, Duarte would certainly have been arrested and ousted as president.

Caught up in the war: peasants carry the body of one of their own back to the farm for burial. (Photo Gary Mark Smith / www.streetphoto.com, CC BY-SA 3.0)

# NOTES

### Introduction
1. Joseph Frazier: *El Salvador Could Be Like That: A Memoir of War, Politics and Journalism on the Front-Row of the Last Bloody Conflict of the US–Soviet Cold War.* (Karina Library Press, 2013)

### Chapter 1
1. smallwarsjournal.com/documents/cale.pdf, Major Paul P. Cale, United States Army

### Chapter 3
1. AbScam, explained Drenkowski, who ended his career in California as a district attorney, was an FBI sting operation designed to ferret out corruption within American politics. Eventually, as he told me, seven congressmen were convicted of accepting bribes from what they thought were Arab lobbyists, hence the name 'Arab Scam' or AbScam. Following that scandal, an enraged Congress, howling about civil liberties or privacy rights, made laws that protected them from certain 'intrusive observations', but not protecting the public, whom they allegedly were protecting. As I understand all this, the FBI and other law enforcement agencies were prohibited from ever bugging or wiretapping the offices of congressmen during investigations of criminal activity.

### Chapter 6
1. Dr Martin Brass, *Soldier of Fortune* magazine in an article headed 'Death to Tyrants'. (September 2007)
2. All that took place in 1984. SOCOM stands for Special Operations Command, at the time stationed in Panama. It was moved to MacDill Air Force Base Florida in 1988 and became part of Joint Special Operations Command (JSOC), with control of all special operations worldwide. JSOC is made up of all special operations units from the US Army, US Navy, US Marine Corps and the US Air Force.

# BIBLIOGRAPHY

Allman, T. D., *Unmanifest Destiny: New York* (Doubleday & Co., 1984)

Alvarez, Roberto, et al, 'Report on Human Rights in El Salvador' (Vintage Books, New York 1982)

Anderson, Thomas P., *Matanza: El Salvador's Communist Revolt of 1932* (University of Nebraska Press, Lincoln, 1971)

Arbuckle, Tammy, 'El Salvador's Bad Example', *Jane's International Defense Review* (May 1990) pp. 8-11.

Bacevich, A. J., et al, *American Military Policy in Small Wars: The Case of El Salvador* (Institute for Foreign Policy, Washington DC, 1988)

Casteen, Charles, *Born in Blood and Fire: A Concise History of Latin America* (Fourth Edition) (W. W. Norton & Co., 2016)

Ching, Erik, *Stories of Civil War in El Salvador: A Battle over Memory* (University of North Carolina Press, 2016)

Corum, James S., 'The Air War in El Salvador', *Aerospace Power Journal* (Summer 1998)

Didion, Joan, *Salvador* (Simon & Schuster, 1983)

Flintham, Victor, *Air Wars and Aircraft: A Detailed Record of Air Combat, 1945 to the Present* (Arms & Armour Press, 1989)

Forum of LAAHS.com website

Haggerty, Richard A., ed., *El Salvador: A Country Study* (Department of the Army, Washington, 1990)

Hennelly, Michael J., 'U.S. Policy in El Salvador: Creating Beauty or the Beast?' *Parameters*, XXIII No. 1 (Spring 1993) pp. 59-69.

Kagan, Robert, 'Remember Nicaragua?' *The Weekly Standard* (25 March 1996) pp. 21-25.

Kissinger, Henry, *White House Years* (Little, Brown & Co., 1979)

Lacefield, Patrick, et al, eds., *El Salvador: Central America in the New Cold War* (Grove Press, New York, 1981)

Lippman, Thomas W., 'Christopher Finds New Latin America', *Washington Post* (29 February 1996) p. A17.

Manwaring, Max G., & Prisk, Courtney, *El Salvador at War: An Oral History from the 1979 Insurrection to the Present* (National Defense University Press, Washington, DC, 1988)

Manwaring, Max, 'Strategic Country Assessment: El Salvador' (US SOUTHCOM, 1988)

Montgomery, Tommie Sue, *Revolution in El Salvador: Origins and Evolution* (Westview Press, Colorado, 1982)

Nixon, Richard, *The Memoirs of Richard Nixon* (Grosset & Dunlap, 1978)

O'Neil, Bard E., *Insurgency & Terrorism* (Brassey's Inc., Washington, 1990)

Pacco, John, *World's Air Forces* (J. P. Publications, 1992)

Macksey, Kenneth & Woodhouse, William, *The Penguin Encyclopaedia of Modern Warfare* (Penguin Group, 1991)

Rosello, Victor M., 'Lessons from El Salvador.' *Parameters*, XXIII No. 4 (Winter 1993–1994) pp. 100-108.

Skipper, Charles O., *El Salvador After 1979: Forces in the Conflict* (Marine Corps Command and Staff College, Virginia,1984)

Willis, David, ed., *Aerospace Encyclopaedia of World Air Forces* (Aerospace Publishing, 1999)

# ACKNOWLEDGEMENTS

I have covered quite a few wars during the course of a career that spans almost half a century, and reckon that what I experienced in El Salvador during its troubles late last century was among the most unsettling. This was not something crazy in Africa or the Middle East: these were good people, brother sometimes fighting brother and very occasionally fathers and sons on opposite sides. It was a tragic illustration of what happens in a society where the economy gets skewered with politics, in this case with an unhealthy infusion of Soviet ideology among rebels trying to unseat the government.

Still, it happened and that is how I met Harry Claflin, an illustrious American marine who had spent two tours with US Marine Reconnaissance in I Corps when he ran that side of things along the Cambodian and Laotian borders. Harry, as the reader will soon discover, had his own views on what was going on in Central America. Without him, this publication would not have appeared.

Another old friend who came up trumps was Dana Drenkowski, a former US Air Force pilot who flew 200 combat missions over Vietnam in B-52 bombers and F4 Phantoms. After Vietnam Dana went on to spend time fighting rebels in Rhodesia's war and then did a bit of odd-job work for Libya's Muammar Gadaffi.

But it was in El Salvador that this erstwhile Californian district attorney was to fine-tune his intelligence skills by keeping certain agencies in Washington abreast of what was going on 'down south'. Dana also provided some of the photos he took on combat ops over those Central American jungles.

For all that, nothing would have happened had my very good friend, former US Army Vietnam veteran Lieutenant Colonel Robert K. Brown – editor and publisher of *Soldier of Fortune* magazine – not provided assistance when I asked him to take me into El Salvador with one of his teams. I had hosted Bob often enough in southern Africa's conflicts and he repaid me tenfold. Thanks, old buddy.

One member of Brown's team who was there at the time was the late Bob MacKenzie, a veteran of US Special Forces in Vietnam and subsequently the Rhodesian SAS where he made captain. Bob was my squad leader on ground patrols in the east of the country. So was Paul Foley, who had spent a dozen years in the French Foreign Legion and sadly, who has also recently taken the Long Walk.

## El Salvador

Accompanying us on these operations was a youthful First Lieutenant Carlos Alfredo Soto. Enterprising and enthusiastic for the survival of his country, he would probably have made staff rank by now had he stayed in the force.

Among a plethora of source material quoted, I am grateful to Major Paul P. Cale for seminal research which was published under the title 'The United States Military Advisory Group in El Salvador, 1979–1992'. And also to Joseph Frazier, author *of El Salvador Could be Like That*, for an objective look at events from someone who observed things from up close. That was underscored by comments made about Frazier's book by Scott Wallace, author of *The Unconquered: In Search of the Amazon's Last Uncontacted Tribes.*

I have quoted liberally from a report titled 'From Madness to Hope: The 12-year War in El Salvador: Report of the Commission on the Truth for El Salvador'. Published by the United States Institute of Peace, I refer specifically to what appeared under the heading 'Death Squad Assassinations'.

The author is flanked by *Soldier of Fortune* magazine's Colonel Robert K. Brown (right) and John Donovan (left). In the background with rifle slung is Vietnam and Rhodesian SAS veteran Bob MacKenzie, KIA in Sierra Leone. (Photo Alwyn Kumst)

# ABOUT THE AUTHOR

Al J. Venter is a specialist military writer who has had fifty books published. He started his career with Geneva's Interavia Group, then owners of *International Defence Review*, to cover military developments in the Middle East and Africa. Venter has been writing on these and related issues such as guerrilla warfare, insurgency, the Middle East and conflict in general for half a century. He was involved with Jane's Information Group for more than thirty years. He was a stringer for the BBC, NBC News (New York), as well as London's *Daily Express* and *Sunday Express*. He branched into television work in the early 1980s, producing more than 100 documentaries, many of which were internationally flighted. His one-hour film, *Africa's Killing Fields*, on the Ugandan civil war, was shown nationwide in the United States on the PBS network. Other films include an hour-long programme on the fifth anniversary of the Soviet invasion of Afghanistan, as well as *AIDS: The African Connection*, which was nominated for China's Pink Magnolia Award. His last major book was *Portugal's Guerrilla Wars in Africa*, nominated in 2013 for New York's Arthur Goodzeit military history book award. It has gone into three editions, including translation into Portuguese.

*El Salvador*